Praise for *Harvesting Your Journals*

"This is a book that honors the journey and the winding path of any of us trying to write our way home. It is a playful, sincere, and encouraging guide to mining the past for revealing patterns. Beneath the clutter of everyday thoughts, Alison Strickland and Rosalie Deer Heart find seeds of wisdom in the private journals they've kept over time. Revealing their own process of writing and growth, the authors share lessons they've learned through journaling, both alone and in creative collaboration. An inspiring book for anyone eager to reap what they've sown and harvest the wisdom they've gained through the years."

— Jan Phillips

Author of *Marry Your Muse: Making a Lasting Commitment to Your Creativity*

"Every bit as valuable for men as it is for women. A great resource. I'm eager to start harvesting my journals."

— Alfred DePew

Author of *The Melancholy of Departure* and journal workshop leader

"This book is a great idea! Finally I have something to offer when my students ask me, 'What do I do with all these volumes?'"

— Christina Baldwin

Author of *Life's Companion: Journal Writing As a Spiritual Quest* and *Calling the Circle: The First and Future Culture*

Also by Rosalie Deer Heart:

Healing Grief: A Mother's Story

Soul Empowerment: A Guidebook for Healing Yourself and Others

Also by Alison Strickland:

Why Can't He Be Mine?

Washington, DC: A Look Around Our Nation's Capital

Getting Rid of Robert

That Doggone Dog!

Harvesting Your Journals

Writing Tools to Enhance Your Growth & Creativity

Rosalie Deer Heart

AND

Alison Strickland

HEART LINK PUBLICATIONS
Santa Fe, New Mexico

PUBLISHED BY: **Heart Link Publications**
PO Box 31280
Santa Fe, NM 87594

EDITOR: Ellen Kleiner
BOOK DESIGN AND PRODUCTION: V. S. Elliott
COVER DESIGN AND PRODUCTION: Christinea Johnson
FRONT COVER PHOTOGRAPH: Jan Phillips
BACK COVER PHOTOGRAPH: Ted Coulson

Printed in the United States of America

Publisher's Cataloging-in-Publication Data

Heart, Rosalie Deer, 1944–
      Harvesting your journals : writing tools to enhance
      your growth and creativity, by Rosalie Deer Heart and
      Alison Strickland. — 1st ed.
            p. cm.
      Includes bibliographical references.
      Preassigned LCCN: 98-73268
      ISBN: 0-9651576-2-8

      1. Self-help techniques. 2. Diaries — Authorship.
3. Creative ability. 4. Self-actualization
(Psychology) I. Strickland, Alison. II. Title.

BF632.H44 1999   158.1
                                  QB198-1173

10 9 8 7 6 5 4 3 2 1

For journal keepers everywhere...

In Gratitude...

We wish to acknowledge our twenty-year friendship, which has deepened through the process of writing this book together. In spite of the challenges and frustrations that arose, as they do each time two people agree to birth a creation together, we always listened and supported each other as we wrote our way home.

We delight in acknowledging our four readers, who generously offered their time, critiques, and love as this book took form: Mel Marsh, Virginia Laken, Elaine Bowman, and Nancy Wilson.

We also extend gratitude to Jan Phillips, Susan Tiberghien, and Eunice Scarfe for mentoring us through the beginnings of this book.

Many thanks to our book-birthing team: Ellen Kleiner, our editor; Christinea Johnson, our cover designer; and SunFlower Elliott, our production wizard.

In addition, Rosalie expresses appreciation to her partner, Michael Bradford, who offered her the solitude to write, open arms when comfort was needed, and sharp eyes for proofreading. Alison extends gratitude to her husband and partner, Ted Coulson, who believed in her and cheerfully gave unfailing support each step of the way.

Contents

Preface

This book took root as we culled through forty years' worth of combined journal writing — a project we decided to undertake in the midst of a rambling poolside conversation one autumn afternoon. "What? You're actually going back through all those dusty journals?" our friends asked, upon hearing of our commitment. "Why would you want to do *that*?" Fair question! And one we occasionally asked ourselves as we worked our way through the process.

Here are our answers. In the beginning we wanted to do it because we had scattered lots of "thought seeds" in our journals. We hoped to see which ones had grown into hardy plants and which had withered and died. Of those that languished, we wondered if they had simply decayed as a result of our changing perspectives or if, out of neglect, their shoots had returned to the soil, perhaps fertilizing other crops.

We had also planted many questions in our journals and wanted to find out which ones were annuals, flowering for one season only; which were perennials, reappearing season after season; and which were evergreens, seemingly always with us, growing larger year by year. We wanted to see how answers had emerged, blossomed, and seeded new questions, and to look for answers that proved so true they became principles that guide us still.

In addition, we wanted to deepen the grasp on our personal histories and map the turning points of our lives — choices made, paths followed, trails abandoned. In the process, we hoped to uncover the patterns in our lives which, like those of crop circles, can be seen only from a distance.

Now we can truly say we found all that, for we discovered new meaning in the seemingly random events of our lives, subtle strands we had not noticed in the busyness of the weaving. With this discovery came a much greater sense of direction, coherence, and purpose than we'd had before.

While sifting through the yellowing pages, we also came upon un-expected bounties. Rereading the old entries seemed to pollinate the journals we continued to keep; even stories, poems, and books sprouted from those seeds planted long ago. Page after page had us reliving precious moments, recovering long-buried memories, appreciating the many ways in which we had ripened over time. In response we deepened our conversations with ourselves and others, further cultivated our friendship with each other, and perhaps more than anything else, developed enormous respect for journaling.

We trust that the experiences, tools, and strategies described in the chapters of this book will help you trace the growth of seeds planted in your journals, whether you have a huge stack of them or only the beginnings of your very first one. We hope that as you harvest your journals you will gain new appreciation for the changing seasons of *your* life, where you've been, and where you yearn to go. We encourage you to use your journals as a rich resource for growing memoirs, essays, or anything else you long to create. And if in the process you celebrate your journey and find new purpose in your writing practice, this book will have more than served its purpose.

Introduction

*H*ave you ever asked yourself if keeping a journal is worth the time and effort it takes? Do you feel an urge to reread your journals, but at a loss about how to begin or what to do with the material you've dug up? Have you tried rereading your journals, only to give up for one reason or another? Would you like to gain fresh insights into yourself? Do you seek inspiration for new creative work? If any of these concerns have crossed your mind in recent months, it may well be time to harvest your journals!

This book is designed to help you each step of the way. As such, it contains some unusual ingredients. You will find, for example, a plenitude of writing exercises — marked by stalks of ripened wheat — to help you discover more about yourself and your life while working with your journals. You will also come across selected journal entries we unearthed, as well as writing we did based on these entries and on the exercises. Along the way you will find dialogues as well, to illustrate the processing you may undergo, both internally and externally.

The following dialogue, for instance, revealing the story of how we embarked on our shared interest in journal keeping, will give you a quick peek into who we are.

ALISON: After twenty-one years, I still laugh about how we met. There I sat in the cafeteria at the Creative Problem Solving Institute (CPSI), quietly eating lunch and you sit down across the table from me and order me to come to your journal keeping workshop that afternoon!

ROSALIE: You had your workshop schedule out, so I figured you hadn't yet decided which one to attend. And I knew you should be with me that day.

ALISON: And you were right. I knew the minute you told me you would be leading a journal keeping workshop that I really did belong there. I'd kept a journal before and wanted to begin again, because I sure had a bunch of stuff to figure out. You must have sensed how confused and troubled I felt — after all, you *are* a bit intuitive!

ROSALIE: I recognized your spirit, and I knew you needed to invest more time and energy in your self-expression and creativity.

ALISON: I knew that, too. I had looked forward to returning to CPSI for months, hoping it would help me figure out where I wanted to go with my life. Then early in the week I wondered why I'd come back. Instead of the clarity I'd hoped to find, I felt more confused than ever. My desperate need to clear space for myself conflicted with my deep concern for my children. I feared I'd ruin my life and theirs.

ROSALIE: Tough place. I know — I've been there.

ALISON: You know what I remember most about that workshop? You said, "To reach the kingdom of the sun, you must spend time in the valley of darkness. If you don't, how will you know the difference?" I held tight to those words over lots of years.

ROSALIE: We've both lived that one more than once!

ALISON: I found another quote in the notes I took that day. You said, "A journal represents an inner response to outer events." Somehow I knew that keeping a journal could help me sort out my life. At the closing session that year, we listed what we planned to do next, and at the top of my list I put, "Buy a blank journal." I had to settle for a college-ruled notebook, because I couldn't find a real journal.

ROSALIE: You can find them easily now, especially in bookstores. It must mean that lots of journal keepers have joined us since.

ALISON: I remember writing to you soon after I got home to thank you and offer to coordinate a workshop in Florida if you'd come. It took a while, but we finally pulled it off. I remember how amazed I felt when you arrived. We'd not spent any time to-gether since that day in your workshop, but when you walked into my home, I felt like I'd known you all my life. That's getting close to the truth now, because we've been good friends for a third of it!

ROSALIE: We shared similar passions — teaching, writing, and living an authentic life. Of course we connected like old friends.

ALISON: Actually, I knew from the beginning we were soul sisters. And I was right!

If you are anything like us, you will want a guide to the lay of the land, which is the reason for this book. Part I, "Entering the Fields," offers numerous strategies and exercises you can start using right away. Part II, "Reaping the Succulence," presents techniques for gathering in meaningful material found in one journal or several of them. Part III, "Bundling the Sheaves," contains collections of journal entries that explore some of the themes we tracked. Drop in and out of this segment of the book as you organize your own themes, reading the chapters in any order you wish and returning to them as desired; each one ends with an invitation to write. Part IV, "Celebrating the Bounties," assists in honoring the work you have completed and in preparing for what may come next.

In conclusion, we offer some words of caution before entering the fields, since they may be infested with pests intent on frightening you away. Only a few days into rereading our journals, we were alarmed by how hard this task really was. "I know exactly what you're going through," a close friend remarked. "I tried rereading my earliest journals, but I got so sick of listening to myself obsess about the same old shit that I quit!" From that moment on, we called the phenomenon, "Oh no — not that shit again!"

The more we talked about harvesting, the more stories we heard about people who had succumbed to the "Oh no's" for one reason or another. "It got too boring," some said, or "I couldn't stand wading through all that self-pitying crap!" or "It depressed me to relive the bad times." One woman became so disgusted with her "immature complaining" and "simplistic thinking" of years gone by that she'd burned all her journals. A middle-aged man not only destroyed his journals but stopped writing altogether. A woman who had followed her therapist's "orders" to ritualistically burn her journals as a way of letting go of the past found it didn't work. Not only was she unable to forget about her wounds but, unable to access her recorded memories, she had lost an important channel leading to resolution, forgiveness, and gratitude.

The message emerging from these stories is, Give in to "Oh no" and you're likely to give up. Give up and you may lose the possibility of understanding yourself better, appreciating yourself more, and developing your writing — all gleanings of a rich and nourishing harvest.

To counteract the "Oh no's" you will undoubtedly experience, here are nine remedies, each of which has been proved effective.

ANTIDOTE #1: REMEMBER YOUR PURPOSE

Write what you hope to gain from the harvest on the cover of the journal you are keeping your notes in. Convert it into a poster to hang where you usually work with your journals.

FROM THE INSIDE COVER OF ALISON'S 1993 JOURNAL:

Beginning a new journal... During my morning writing ritual, I tune in to discover more of myself, clarify my vision, play with possibilities. Sometimes it's shining, free flowing, and fun. Other times it's whiny, sluggish, and miserable. Always, it's valuable. It's all grist for the creative mill. It keeps the lines of communication open between my conscious mind and daily life and my less conscious, timeless self — the source of insights and new understanding. It also keeps the writing muscles limber and strong.

ANTIDOTE #2: EXPECT AN "OH NO" EXPERIENCE, AND PERSEVERE

Smile, and remember that most often your writing is much better than you think.

FROM ROSALIE'S JOURNAL:

Whenever I avoid writing by escaping into housework or meaningless conversations, or grocery shopping even though the refrigerator is bulging with food, I know a truth is struggling to emerge. Resistance is like a weed I pull out once and assume its life is over. But in personal growth, as in gardening, seldom is this the case.

ANTIDOTE #3: BE GENTLE WITH YOURSELF

Honor the person you were at the time. You could even write a message of appreciation to the person you were when you began to write a journal.

FROM ALISON'S NOTES:
While rereading entries, especially the earliest ones, I sometimes had to curb my impatience with the woman I was. Instead of honoring how much I'd grown, I judged the woman who poured so much confusion and fear into college-ruled notebooks. Then I decided to sit beside her as an older, wiser friend who could understand her longing for change and appreciate just how brave she was to keep on asking hard questions and imagining a richer life. I envisioned myself sitting beside her as she wrote, and whispering, "Thank you for being so brave."

As I read, I imagined I could actually go back to comfort and encourage the sometimes confused, fearful, always yearning and questioning younger woman I found in my early journals. I told her not only how brave she was but that she had proved worthy of her quest, and I explained that everything she worried about was going to turn out just fine. I assured her that unexpected magic lay ahead, and I thanked her again for setting forth courageously on her journey, for without her courage, I'd never have become the woman I am today.

ANTIDOTE #4: TRUST THE PROCESS

Remember that fallow periods precede the appearance of new sprouts. By the same token, sporadic or sluggish attentiveness to journal writing often gives way to a good, creative flow. What counts is showing up no matter what and keeping your pen moving.

FROM ROSALIE'S JOURNAL:
I'm catching on. When I don't want to face myself, I don't write. If I don't see my pain on paper, I am able to deny it.

ANTIDOTE #5: LOOK FOR THE BIGGER PICTURE

When you think you are running around in circles, realize you're actually spiraling, learning lessons that take you higher with each round.

FROM ROSALIE'S JOURNAL:

I grieve the distance separating me from my soul. The writing flow has halted, most likely because I have stopped meditating and exercising. Once again, I have to learn the same lesson. When I consciously focus my energies, I am aware of light; when I retract my energies, I am aware of darkness. My intention makes all the difference.

ANTIDOTE #6: PERSIST

When you know you're whining or resisting reading the "same old shit," read it anyway — right through your stuck place. You'll most often find a treasure waiting on the other side.

FROM ALISON'S JOURNAL:

Why do we think life lessons should be learned once and for all in one shining moment of insight, one epiphany of awareness that suddenly transforms us forever? Of course not — that's only the beginning. The transformation isn't complete until we can live the insight naturally, without thinking about it. And when it's become that much a part of us, I suppose rereading the initial flash in an old journal might sound banal, ordinary as yesterday's news.

ANTIDOTE #7: PLAY "WHAT'S GOOD ABOUT IT?"

Seek out the benefits any time you feel resistance while rereading. Be creative!

Here's Rosalie playing what's-good-about-it after rereading an entry written just after her divorce:

Writing helped me map the grief journey. Not even with close friends did I share all the pain I felt from so much loss and internal erosion; I reserved the litanies of loneliness for my journal. What's good about it is that I released some of the suffering through my words. What's good about it is that I broke my silence.

And here's Alison responding to the vanishing of her muse:

My muse can get fickle. Sometimes when I call she shows right up and gifts me with words that surprise and delight me. Other times she seems to desert me, vanishing without a trace. Maybe she's gone shopping! When I call and there's no answer, I sit empty-headed without inspiration or imagination, worrying that she never really existed, that it's silly to believe in her, let alone wait for her to show up.

This gray morning, I called her to help me get started writing: "OK muse, where are you? I'm trying to keep up my end of the bargain. I'm faithful in the morning. Come on, talk to me!"

I listen; there's only silence. I drift with the music of *Secret Garden*. I feel my eyes burning. I feel abandoned and bereft sitting alone in echoing silence. As my laptop hums away, the music gets sadder. I sit. I wait. I won't give up. I relax my body and allow my mind to follow the melody so filled with longing. I listen for her words....

OK, so she didn't show up! What's the big deal? What I wrote reads well and it's honest. No optimistic platitudes here! And I can take full credit for it 'cause she never showed up. Maybe she just wants to remind me that I can go it alone.

ANTIDOTE #8: COLLECT THE THOUGHTS OF OTHER WRITERS AS REMINDERS THAT YOU'RE NOT ALONE

"Talk" to published writers. Add your voice to theirs.

Alison often talks to other writers in her journal, sometimes responding to their printed words. She wrote this commentary soon after she began "goofing off" instead of vigorously continuing her harvesting work.

A quote I want to remember from reading *Everyday Sacred* by Sue Bender: "Why are there times when I don't know, and it doesn't seem to matter, and times when not knowing fills me with dread? 'To suffer one's confusion is the first step in healing,' I read. I was relieved."

Me, too... reminds me that harvesting is healing. I'm much more patient with myself than I was when I began.

ANTIDOTE #9: GET SUPPORT FOR YOUR HARVESTING

Harvesting can be lonely, challenging work. If you have a life partner, take time to explain what you're doing and why it's important to you. If not, find at least one harvesting "buddy" you can confide in. If you know several journal keepers, form a harvesting community. Meet regularly to affirm one another, read favorite passages, and share insights and discoveries.

Together, develop easy-to-remember guidelines to follow. First, insist on confidentiality. Second, come together to listen deeply and bear witness to one another, not to critique or psychoanalyze. Third, allow everyone the right to pass on their turn — without reading aloud or commenting.

Eunice Scarfe, a writer and teacher who skillfully creates safe environments for sharing, suggests the following approaches to commenting on the writing of others:

"I *liked the wording (sequencing) of* _____."

"I *was wondering about* _____, *because I noticed myself* _____."

"*Listening to you read, I was feeling (sensing, thinking, responding to)* _____."

She also cautions listeners not to tell their versions of the story. The rendering remains the sole task of the storyteller.

If a writing circle does not mesh with your current lifestyle, perhaps a trusted friend can support you. Share your discoveries with this person. Read aloud segments of your journals, and invite your confidante to dialogue about the issues you're exploring. Explain the sort of feedback that would help you most.

Now the time has come to begin your harvest...

PART I

Entering the Fields

Stepping into Your Journals

Armed with antidotes in case you encounter pests, it is time to enter the fields. Ahead lie helpful tips about attitudes and actions that contribute to a bountiful harvest. Beyond you'll find tools to use as you read a journal. And so the harvest begins.

1

Ways to Be

*T*he spirit in which we approach what we do determines how we do it and, in many cases, whether we do it at all! Hence it is a good idea, as you enter the fields of your journals, to take along a list of "ways to be." Why? Because the attitudes brought to harvesting can make all the difference in the world, contributing to an easier workload and a more bountiful yield.

Before beginning your list, think of the qualities that support the rereading of your journal entries. Notice what interferes with your concentration and invent ways to work around it. Remember, these will be guidelines, not rules; as such, they may change from week to week. More than anything else, trust your own knowing.

The following strategies are grounded in principles of creativity and spiritual growth. Consider adding to your "ways to be" list those that apply, and leave the rest behind.

Committed

We live in a busy world, with demands coming at us from all direc-tions. Always, there is something else to do and someone else to attend to. Amid the myriad of tasks that compete for our time and attention, dedication is essential.

FROM ROSALIE'S JOURNAL:
Will working with my journals be forever postponed to a time when there are no dishes or clothes to wash, no child to care for, no telephone to answer? For two decades I have grounded myself by

setting pen to paper, yet I have not taken this urge to write seriously. When I am not distracted from this task by others, I find ways to distract myself.

To encourage yourself to work consistently and undistractedly with your old journals, tell yourself, "I am worth it!" After all, investing time and energy in reviewing your journals is a commitment to *yourself*. It's not selfish, although others may try to convince you it is. To the contrary, the discoveries you make and the insights you gain will nourish and enrich your life. The fruits of your harvest will nourish others too.

With this in mind, think of ways to remind yourself that you are worthy of immersing yourself in your journals. Many writers use affirmations, for example, to remain focused on their writing. You, too, may benefit from affirmations. At the very least, write down three things you will do to honor your commitment to harvesting.

Curious

Walking back into the past can stir feelings of regret that may quickly turn into blame and judgment — of yourself and others. Ditch blame and judgment; they destroy self-worth and kill creativity. Instead, pore over your writings with a spirit of curiosity and discovery. This will awaken your imagination and nourish your creativity, both of which will expand your capacity to learn.

Listen to Rosalie's words written in her journal in December 1976, after an unwanted emergency hysterectomy:
I feel ashamed. I hate to complain to friends, so I whine in secret and write in my journal. I torture myself with decrees that I should be stronger, or at least more objective. I'm angry and discouraged. I don't know where my voice is. Questions of life and death continue to invade my consciousness. I resent this cruel interruption of my life.

One month later she wrote:
What replenishes me most of all is writing. When I write, I see myself more clearly and gradually forgive myself.

While rereading your journals, you'll be encountering parts of yourself that can then be gathered in to make you more whole. Valuable insights will also come your way, provided that you remind yourself to think flexibly and try out new perspectives. If you gather regrets, transform them into teachers and learn from them. Also take in your hopes and fears, noting how they've changed over time and, in the process, changed you.

For many people, delving into the spirit of curiosity takes practice. One way to start is by remembering something you regret, whether you wrote about it or not. Now think of it as a lesson sent to you by a wise teacher who had your best interests at heart. List the lessons you learned, even if you are still learning them!

Humorous

Learning from your life is a task that deserves to be enjoyed, so take the work seriously and yourself lightly. Turn tragedies into comedies. Look for comic moments. If you missed them at the time, revel in them now! And as you work, remember to laugh; laughter nourishes creativity. Try exaggerating your woes until they crack you up. Play "Ain't if awful!" till you can't help but laugh.

Objective and Compassionate

Enter the fields of your journals with the objectivity of a historian and the compassion of a trusted friend or spiritual advisor. Moving back and forth between objectivity and compassion will keep you balanced and protect you from falling into blame and judgment. To enliven both these personae in your imagination, talk with them as you work. Ask your historian to help you take the long view; and let your compassionate companion open your heart to everyone you encounter in your journals, including yourself.

FROM ALISON'S JOURNAL:
I know I have much to add to the growing chorus of women's voices, yet this morning I sit here filled with doubt. All these years of writing and so little published work to show for it. Muse, I think we need to talk!

Yes, remember when you found in the margin of a journal you fin-
ished years ago these words written in your own hand: "You will
do your REAL *work, your most important work, after you're sixty"?*
Well, I wrote that. I put that there for you to find when you needed
it most. It's your time, babe! You've sowed your seeds, and now
the field's ripe for harvest and you are ready!

Confident

Above all, be confident in the harvesting process. Remember, there's
no way to do it wrong; there's only *your way.*

A MESSAGE FROM ALISON'S MUSE:

Remember and believe. Trust your process. When you do that,
words flow once more. Remember, you're harvesting many years of
longing to write, not realizing you already were. Like a pilgrim in your
own backyard, you've wandered and questioned and delighted and
rejoiced as well. And now the struggle eases, the path is cleared,
and you know what to do should the fog roll in!

Thinking back over the ideas that came to you while reading this
chapter, list the ways you want to be while proceeding with your
harvest. Take into account your most important issues, stating them
in positive terms rather than as areas to avoid. When your list is
complete, post it in the spot where you are apt to be rereading your
journals. Review this list periodically, especially when you are feeling
discouraged by or resistant to the material you unearth.

2

Things to Do

Here are some steps you can take to maintain your momentum as you make your way through the fields of your journals. We found each one of them effective and offer them simply as possibilities to play with.

Create a Special Place for Doing the Work

It helps to have a quiet, comfortable place for foraging. The more inviting your spot is, the more likely you'll be to go there. Begin by asking yourself what sort of environment helps you focus your attention, then turn on your imagination as you furnish your special place with tools of the trade and elements that inspire.

Here's what we did. Alison has a study where she keeps all her journals and books about writing, sticky notes, colored markers, and special pens. But she only worked there when the weather kept her away from her writing place by her backyard pool. If she had to work inside, she wanted music, fresh flowers, and candles nearby.

Rosalie, a gypsy at heart, set up camp wherever she happened to be. Whatever her destination was, music accompanied her harvesting. She also toted a portable water fountain that reminded her to be fluid as she gathered material from her journals.

Actually, this work can happen almost anywhere. We've both harvested journals in airports and airplanes, hotel rooms, hospital waiting rooms, at the beach, and in cafes.

Make Appointments with Yourself and Keep Them

Give yourself the time you need for this work on a regular basis. In other words, schedule time with yourself just as you do with doctors, accountants, clients, and others. If you live with a housemate or family members, you may need to negotiate for both time and privacy — then show up!

Commit to checking in with yourself. Taking time to create something whole and meaningful from the fragments of your life is every bit as important as tending to the other appointments marked on your calendar! Whereas Alison designated entire weekends to foraging, Rosalie blocked off hours on specific days and tacked a note on her door, which read *Do Not Disturb*.

Decide on Where to Store Your Harvest

Where will you keep your harvest? That depends on your intention and purpose. If your goal is to look for patterns and gather insights, you may want to keep a separate journal for your harvesting thoughts. If you hope to gather material to share with others, try transcribing segments onto a computer. Perhaps you know exactly where you want to record your thinking. If not, experiment until you find what works for you.

A combination of strategies may be the answer. Alison, for example, began collecting prize quotes and short segments in a small spiral-bound notebook she now calls her Nuggets Journal. In a separate computer file she gathered stories about her two young grandchildren so that someday she could write a book of childhood stories for them.

Take Breaks

There's no need to work your way nonstop through all your journals, especially if you have many to reread. In fact, it's often a good idea to take a break along the way.

Any time you feel an urge to stop, ask yourself, "Is this resistance or is a time for a breather?" If it's resistance — a feeling you will recognize by a familiar tightening of the stomach, a sense of anxiety, or the inclination to convince yourself that you're too tired, too confused, or too narcissistic — muster up courage to override it. If it's time for a breather, take a break. Chapters 5 and 6 offer strategies for completing what you've done and for returning to the harvest when you're ready.

Keep It Fun

Harvesting doesn't have to be all serious introspection! Find ways to make it fun by experimenting with different approaches. For example, connect your harvest with other creative pursuits you enjoy. Or when you've finished rereading a journal, make a collage of images that reflect the contents, and glue it on the cover or use it as a book jacket. Or design a booklet of irresistible morsels you've found, and illustrate each one with a photograph or a sketch. The point is to enjoy, create, and celebrate.

3

Summoning Courage

*H*arvesting requires courage. People may convince you that you're wasting your time. Other projects may distract you. You may even distract yourself! Once you have sat down to reread and reflect on your journals, you may feel an urge to fix a snack or call a friend. Or you may begin yawning and decide you're too tired to plunge into a single entry. Or you may be suddenly attacked by those "Oh no " pests.

The exercises in this chapter will help you strengthen your resolve. First you will find a guided meditation designed for courting your muse — your source of inner wisdom. It is she who inspires you, deepens you, and comforts you. Some people refer to her as their angel of encouragement. She gives voice to the receptive, intuitive, feminine side that both men and women have but too often ignore.

Following this meditation are brief listing exercises. The lists you compile will serve as touchstones as you work with your journals, reminding you of who you are, why you write, and what you hope to glean from your harvest. Together, the meditation and listing exercises will spur you on no matter what obstacles may arise in the fields of your journals.

Courting Your Muse

In the spirit of discovery, we invite you to court your muse as you begin harvesting your journals. Whether or not you are already acquainted with your muse, recognize that there is always more to learn about this inspirer. Sometimes it helps to imagine your muse as the silence that exists between thoughts, as a real or imaginary person of wisdom and magic, or as a real or imaginary animal or plant.

Our respective muses are often unpredictable. Rosalie experiences hers as an inner sponsor that is at times a practitioner of tough love and at other times a comforter. Alison's muse came to her unsought years ago, offering to teach her how to translate into words the thoughts that emerged as vague images or heartfelt "knowings" she could only sense kinesthetically. Her muse kept the promise, and sometimes even arrives on a shiny black horse that reminds Alison of the adventurous imagination she had as a horse-crazy young girl.

Before beginning the meditation, it is therefore a good idea to release any assumptions you may have about the form your muse may take, and to trust your initial instincts. Also be sure to have two sheets of paper by your side, as well as a pen or pencil, since after the meditation you will be writing. First, read all the way through the meditation, then close your eyes and let the experience unfold.

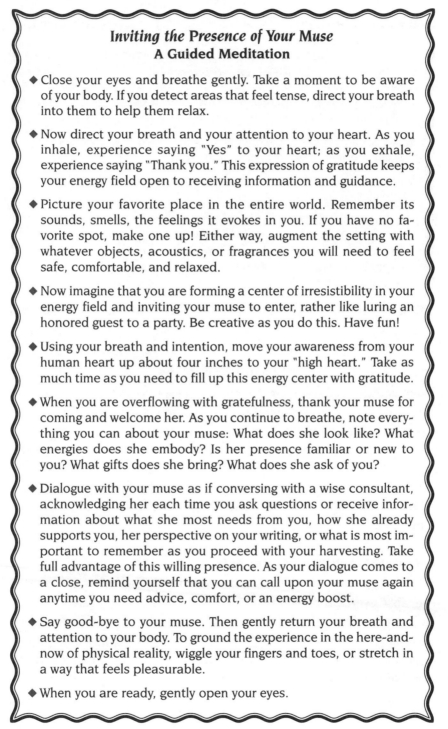

Inviting the Presence of Your Muse
A Guided Meditation

◆ Close your eyes and breathe gently. Take a moment to be aware of your body. If you detect areas that feel tense, direct your breath into them to help them relax.

◆ Now direct your breath and your attention to your heart. As you inhale, experience saying "Yes" to your heart; as you exhale, experience saying "Thank you." This expression of gratitude keeps your energy field open to receiving information and guidance.

◆ Picture your favorite place in the entire world. Remember its sounds, smells, the feelings it evokes in you. If you have no favorite spot, make one up! Either way, augment the setting with whatever objects, acoustics, or fragrances you will need to feel safe, comfortable, and relaxed.

◆ Now imagine that you are forming a center of irresistibility in your energy field and inviting your muse to enter, rather like luring an honored guest to a party. Be creative as you do this. Have fun!

◆ Using your breath and intention, move your awareness from your human heart up about four inches to your "high heart." Take as much time as you need to fill up this energy center with gratitude.

◆ When you are overflowing with gratefulness, thank your muse for coming and welcome her. As you continue to breathe, note everything you can about your muse: What does she look like? What energies does she embody? Is her presence familiar or new to you? What gifts does she bring? What does she ask of you?

◆ Dialogue with your muse as if conversing with a wise consultant, acknowledging her each time you ask questions or receive information about what she most needs from you, how she already supports you, her perspective on your writing, or what is most important to remember as you proceed with your harvesting. Take full advantage of this willing presence. As your dialogue comes to a close, remind yourself that you can call upon your muse again anytime you need advice, comfort, or an energy boost.

◆ Say good-bye to your muse. Then gently return your breath and attention to your body. To ground the experience in the here-and-now of physical reality, wiggle your fingers and toes, or stretch in a way that feels pleasurable.

◆ When you are ready, gently open your eyes.

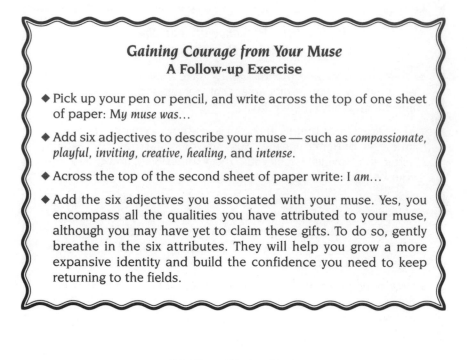

Gaining Courage from Your Muse
A Follow-up Exercise

◆ Pick up your pen or pencil, and write across the top of one sheet of paper: My *muse was...*

◆ Add six adjectives to describe your muse — such as *compassionate, playful, inviting, creative, healing,* and *intense.*

◆ Across the top of the second sheet of paper write: I *am...*

◆ Add the six adjectives you associated with your muse. Yes, you encompass all the qualities you have attributed to your muse, although you may have yet to claim these gifts. To do so, gently breathe in the six attributes. They will help you grow a more expansive identity and build the confidence you need to keep returning to the fields.

Listing Exercises

Here you will be compiling three lists. Before beginning, decide on a place to keep them, preferably a spot where they can be easily retrieved any time you need reminding or want to add to them. If you are keeping a separate harvesting journal, you might want to tuck them behind the front cover. Also be sure to leave plenty of space at the bottom of each list for any additions you may wish to make. Consider turning your lists into "encouragement" posters to display in your special harvesting place.

LIST #1: EXPLORING WHO YOU ARE

Many people who write hesitate to call themselves writers. We know, because even after having several books published we were reluctant to call ourselves writers! Now we believe that if you are called to write and have the courage to set words to paper, you are a writer and are worthy of the name. Understanding why you have chosen to take journal writing seriously will give you courage to continue both the writing and the harvesting.

Complete this sentence by listing everything you know about the writer you already are, including pertinent adjectives from the follow-up exercise on page 32:

I *am a writer who...*

LINES FROM ALISON'S LIST:

~I am a writer who greets the sun with pen in hand.

~I am a writer who craves solitude so that words can find me.

~I am a writer who craves the company of others who write.

~I am a writer who understands that she already knows everything she needs to know if she can just get out of the way enough to listen.

LINES FROM ROSALIE'S LIST:

~I am a writer who enjoys the feel of the edge of my hand touching the blank page as my pen takes flight.

~I am a writer who amuses and amazes myself almost every time I write.

~I am a writer who guards my privacy and writes each day to remain honest and current with myself.

~I am a writer who believes that by writing each day I add to my own peace and well-being, and to the planet's too.

LIST #2: DEFINING WHY YOU WRITE

Being clear about why you write will deepen your resolve to write, especially when the "distraction demons" dance through your mind. Moreover, acknowledging that writing is a source of self-empowerment will create inner momentum even when you are tempted to avoid returning to your journal.

Complete this sentence by listing everything you know about why you write:

I *write to...*

Here are lines from our lists to get you started:

~I write to figure out what I think.

~I write to clear my mind and open my heart.

∿I write to find order in chaos.

∿I write so that I will project less often and be less defensive.

∿I write to explore the deepest, farthest edges of myself.

∿I write to avoid keeping secrets.

∿I write to recognize who and what I need to forgive and make peace with.

∿I write to find my way home to myself.

∿I write to have conversations with my soul.

∿I write to understand smoke signals from the universe.

∿I write to remember joy and name sadness.

LIST #3: SETTING YOUR INTENTIONS AND CLARIFYING YOUR PURPOSE

Before harvesting notes from your past, it's important to set your intentions. The clearer you are about what you want to achieve, the more likely you will be to achieve it. The same is true of purpose. When you are in touch with your purpose, you are more apt to persist in the face of resistance and self-doubt. Since intention and purpose can change as harvesting progresses, leave room on the page for additions and modifications.

Complete the following sentences in as many ways as you like. The thoughts you record will help you clarify your intentions and lead you to purpose:

As I *think about harvesting, I am aware of…*

I *hope to find…*

I *want to achieve…*

I *will know harvesting has been worthwhile when…*

Now reread what you wrote, then complete these two additional sentences. Think of intention as *what* you want to achieve and purpose as *why* you want to achieve it.

My *intention for the harvest is…*

My *purpose is…*

4

Tools for Beginning Your Harvest

*J*ust as farmers enter ripened fields with a variety of hand tools and machines, so can you approach your journals with an assortment of time-tested methods geared for ensuring a successful harvest. Those described below were of greatest benefit to us and the journal keepers we've worked with. In the end, however, only *you* know what's in your journals and what you hope to achieve by reviewing them. So pick and choose from among the following tools those that are most likely to help you glean the rewards you seek, then add some of your own.

Basic Tools

These tools will help you spot the fruits and blossoms hidden in your journals, then mark those you want to bring in from the fields. On page 42 are tools you can use to work each crop until it yields insights and stimulates new ideas.

FOCUSED ATTENTION

Having specific signposts to look for as you reread will help focus your attention and keep you going. At the same time, watch for the unexpected. You are likely to bring back many juicy morsels you did not set out to gather!

To keep your attention sharply focused, bring these three lists into the fields with you. Refer to them any time you feel the need to ground your mission.

LIST #1: THEMES

Jot down the themes you'd like to look for. (Expect them to change as you proceed.) Sample themes include body image, power of place, friendships, dreams, and aging. Be sure to leave plenty of room beneath each item on your list for noting discoveries as they arise. Marking the page numbers or dates of entries containing these discoveries will help you find them later.

LIST #2: QUESTIONS

Record the questions you'd like to find answers to. (Expect these to change, too.) Consider the following: What is the place of joy in my life? What accounts for love? What, for me, is the deeper meaning of inactivity? How do I nourish my soul in the midst of life's demands? What is the difference between taking care of myself and taking care of others? As before, leave ample blank space for the answers you collect.

LIST #3: MOTIFS

Note the more specific motifs you hope to find. Here are some possibilities to help get you started:

- ◆ *Forgotten dreams*
- ◆ *Key turning points — events that you knew changed your life*
- ◆ *Seemingly innocuous choices that turned out to have a huge impact*
- ◆ *Times you circled back and adopted a different perspective*
- ◆ *Uncovered memories you never want to forget again*
- ◆ *Events you didn't write about*
- ◆ *Times of connection and instances of separation*
- ◆ *Sacred people, events, conversations, places, rituals, and activities*
- ◆ *Your primary "cast of characters"*
- ◆ *Conversations that stirred you*
- ◆ *Times when you broke your silence and spoke your truth*

LABELING YOUR CROPS

Just as garden markers show you where the basil and oregano grow, so can labels of various sorts identify the thoughts you hope to gather as you read. To begin with, it is a good idea to record on each journal the starting and ending dates of entries it contains. Note where you were if the location is unusual or highly significant.

Colored highlighters work beautifully for marking important passages. In one color, highlight the lines you like. In another, draw bold strokes down the margins of significant paragraphs. Then with a darker fine-line pen, identify your colored markings by theme so that when you return you'll know what they're about. Every now and then you may also want to draw a bold line across the top of a page and add a title summarizing the contents of those entries.

Brightly colored stick-on tabs, found in most office supply stores, can be used to mark important segments. Or to keep things simple, just fold down the corners of pages you want to return to.

If you're feeling extremely ambitious, consider drafting a table of contents for each of your journals and taping it to the top of the first page. In the future you may want to leave a blank page at the front of new journals for this purpose.

WRITING EXERCISES

Some of our journaling strategies quite naturally became an integral part of our harvesting practice. After rereading parts of our journals, we adopted them to connect subthemes and spark new insights and ideas. Any time you want to stop and reflect on what you've read, you can use one or more of these writing tools to interact with the material by writing more. As you work with the tools, don't be surprised if you suddenly find answers to your most vexing questions.

Free Writing

Without stopping, let your penned thoughts about what you've read take you where they will. To prime their writing pump, many people keep the pen moving without stopping to worry about points their former English teachers might have critiqued. Some set a timer and keep writing until it goes off. Others fill a certain number of pages before stopping to rest. The method you use does not matter; the object is to keep your hand moving across the page even if you have to repeat yourself or write, "I don't know what to say next."

TRY THIS: After rereading a journal, finish with a free writing session to record what you remember. Then highlight or tag the parts that interest you most.

Capturing the Now

This exercise, like the previous one, keeps you writing without worrying about form or structure. While capturing the now, however, you focus on what's going on inside you and what's happening around you. Following your awareness moment by moment, you may shift at will from internal events to external ones, and back again. Working with this tool will bring clarity to your awareness as well as your writing, and will keep you grounded in "what is."

TRY THIS: Should you begin ruminating about the past, judging yourself or others, or feeling vaguely uneasy about what you've read, stop, and for at least ten minutes capture the now. You could begin with, "Right now I am aware of..." and return to this phrase whenever you find your thoughts drifting back in time.

Turning Thoughts into Written Dialogues

Harvesting is essentially a dialogue with yourself. Rather than simply picking up fully ripened truths and placing them in your basket, you are *interacting* with the material you find. Converting these interactions into written dialogues is a retrieval and discovery tool you can use with almost anything you've written about — another person, an event, even a dream.

Here Rosalie dialogues with her muse as she begins assembling her themes.

ME: I have so many stories in my heart and psychic womb.

MUSE: Indeed, you have. So why wait? Begin.

ME: I am — by conversing with you. I value your voice, your guidance, your lightness.

MUSE: And don't forget my darkness. I carry that medicine too.

ME: It's a deal. So can you help me begin?

MUSE: Of course. Begin with love — times when you were in love, with love, inviting love.

> Also write about times when love was missing and when love was returned, betrayed, unacknowledged. You know that love honors the sacredness of the soul; you have written about those times in your abbreviated way. Now let's hear the roar of all you know. Trust me to fill in the pauses. I promise to gift you with dreams, visit with you, and guide you to even more love experiences.

ME: I'm ready.

MUSE: Remember, be with love. Write in love.

TRY THIS: If while in the process of rereading your journals you encounter a person with whom you have "unfinished business," bring the individual into your awareness and talk with them. First, take a breath; empty your mind of thoughts, especially notions about how *right* you are; and calm your emotions. Taking another breath, release your perceptions. Then tell the person how you feel now and listen compassionately for their response. Ask questions and listen for their answers. Let the dialogue bounce back and forth between the two of you until you feel finished with it. Before saying good-bye, thank the person for the part they played in your life and tell them what you've learned from having known them.

Making Metaphorical Connections

Thinking metaphorically about events you've described, or your reactions to them, can spark new insights and launch you into unforeseen directions. If you've been told that it's important to differentiate between a simile (an analogy introduced by the word *like* or *as*) and a metaphor (an analogy *not* introduced by *like* or *as*), forget all that and go for the connection. In other words, while writing about your harvesting adventures, play with metaphorical thinking and use *like* and *as* to your heart's content! For instance Alison, having described one segment of an early journal with the simile "like wandering in a maze," later gave it a metaphorical title: "The Time of the Maze."

The title of this book is a metaphor suggesting that reviewing old journals is akin to harvesting a crop. Long before writing it, we spent hours discussing what this metaphor could tell us about the practice we ourselves were immersed in; then later, the metaphor gave us ideas for the structure and content of the book. Aristotle called metaphorical writing "the use of the wrong word on purpose." Marion Woodman, well-known Jungian analyst and prolific writer, believes metaphors heal us and return us to wholeness. With these thoughts in mind, feel free to use the images, words, stories, and dreams you uncover as metaphors for your life.

TRY THIS: While going through your journals, collect the metaphors you used repeatedly. Then pick one and list the qualities it alludes to. Finally, make connections between these qualities and the segments of your life they describe. In short, see what the metaphors you've applied can tell you about yourself.

Alison, in rereading her journals, found numerous references to spirals. She discovered that she'd relied on this image to help her through "stuck places" in her life. The spiral reminded her that growth comes from within; that development moves in cycles; and that running around in circles can gradually take her higher.

Intuitive Writing

Intuitive writing, like free writing, has the hand moving quickly, without censorship. Here, however, you begin by quieting your mind. After entering into silence, allow your hand to record whatever comes next. Try it and see what happens. Don't be alarmed if the words you set down include a request for inner guidance. Your intuition, after all, is the voice of your soul and connects you with your inner wisdom.

FROM ALISON'S NOTEBOOK:

In my earliest journals, I longed to contact deeper parts of myself to reach what I thought of as my higher self. Intellectually, I understood the witness — the part of me that lives beyond ego — but I wanted more than that. I wanted to tap into what Jung called the collective unconscious. In later journals, I learned to listen to the stillness and let the words come. When I eventually began to take myself more seriously as a writer, I initiated conversations with the muse, and she almost always showed up. I would ask her questions; she would answer them. Later, I found that my relationship with her deserved the same passionate commitment as marriage. Now she's not just THE muse; she's MY muse. And I honor her presence each day as I write.

FROM ROSALIE'S NOTES:

For years, "blink truths" came to me. As I began recording them, they would suddenly grow into sentences, then paragraphs, and occasionally entire pages. Sometimes, uninvited words would spill out onto blank pages. Later, I discovered I could ask for information. In time, I learned to have a pen or pencil handy to record guidance whenever and wherever it popped in.

TRY THIS: When in reviewing your journals you come across an unanswered question you had been pondering for some time, work through it with intuitive writing. For maximum effectiveness, approach this exercise with open expectations. Remember, answers cannot be willed; they can only be allowed. So quiet yourself for a few moments, then write the question slowly and thoughtfully. Keeping your hand moving spontaneously, write whatever comes to mind. With practice, you'll sense a shift from what you were wondering about to what you *know* on a deeper level.

Reflective Writing

Alison developed reflective writing years ago to help workshop participants track their key discoveries. To begin, quiet yourself and allow your mind to revisit the experience you want to reflect on, noticing the images, feelings, and words that arise. Then without worrying about spelling or syntax, start capturing your impressions in writing. As in free writing, keep your hand moving and the words flowing onto the page. If your hand slows down, write, "I remember..." and keep going. Write for at least ten minutes.

Reviewing what you've written, highlight any nuggets you find. Then complete these unfinished sentences:

I *learned*...

I *relearned*...

I *discovered*...

I *rediscovered*...

Finally, look for the implications underlying your discoveries by completing these sentences:

I *regret...*

I *appreciate...*

Right now I feel...

And I will...

You can use reflective writing any time you have finished reading a segment or an entire journal. It will also prove enlightening while bundling the themes you've tracked, as is illustrated in Part III.

Additional Tools

After experimenting with the basic tools, you may want to vary your harvesting routine. The tools that follow will help you break new ground and interact with your journals through other forms of writing.

A SEED JOURNAL

From the journal lines you have highlighted, select short segments you love — a phrase, a single line, a few sentences — and compile a running list of them. Then plant each one in a "seed journal" created just for this purpose. Later you can scoop them out and grow new writing from them.

A seed journal can take any form you wish. Rosalie keeps seed files on her laptop, where they wait to inspire her. When someone gave Alison a small journal encased in pastel fabric bearing a swirled abstract design, she began copying onto its marbled pages the passages she cherished most. She imagines having this seed journal at her bedside when she's dying, for it holds the most profound wisdom she's encountered.

OTHER COLLECTIONS

There is great joy in being a collector of your own past thoughts, emotions, and observations. As before, gather the desired material into appropriately designated notebooks, computer files, or journals so that in the future you can find just the morsels you are looking for.

What is there to collect? Any subject matter that recurs throughout the pages of your journals, such as the following:

◆ Metaphors that still speak to you

◆ Sudden moments of insight

◆ "Teachers" who have come into your life

◆ Writers you have admired

◆ Dreams you remember as though you had them yesterday

◆ People you're glad you've met

◆ Ideas that have captivated you

◆ Events that still move you to tears

◆ Celebrations you want to remember

◆ Sorrows that came as teachers bearing gifts

◆ Words with a pulse of their own that still speak to you today

◆ Songs that have special meaning

Collections, like seed journals, hold fodder for future writing. Because their contents tend to be more extensively chronicled, however, they are apt to fertilize your *own* growth as well. Here are a few examples of what you can do with your collections. (For more possibilities, see Part IV.)

Looking over your teacher collection, ask yourself: What do these teachers have in common? How are they different? What was my definition of a good teacher when I was younger? How has it changed? What is it now? Then dialogue — as described on pages 38–39 — with one of your best teachers about what you are learning while harvesting.

From your list of revered writers, create an imaginary writers' circle, then compose the dialogues you would have with them. When Alison was traveling so much she couldn't join a community of writers, she filled the void by calling together a fictional one where she sat and "talked" with authors she valued, recording the conversations in her journal.

Glancing through your collection of words, select one to explore. What does this word have to say to you? What images and memories does it evoke? Recall when you first wrote the word, using it consciously and with intention. What did it mean to you at the time?

Look up the word in a dictionary; what does its origin suggest to you? With all this in mind, write a dialogue with the word.

Here are other growth-promoting activities to try. Pick a bunch of words from your collection and draft a letter to yourself using every one of them. Or write a poem, beginning each line with a word in your collection.

Now that you've scoured the fields and gathered in your harvest, it's time to make better sense of it all and to begin tracking your primary themes. Part II will help you get going so that before long you'll be drawing forth richness and sustenance from these well-tended crops.

Reaping the Succulence

Reflecting on What You Have Gathered

Whether you've finished reading one journal or returned from the fields with crops gathered from quite a few, further reflection brings more nourishment and growth. Here you will find strategies for working with your crops until they yield great sustenance.

5

Techniques to Use with One Journal

Who was I before, and who am I now? Which of my struggles and aspirations remain the same, and which ones have I outgrown? Where might I be tomorrow? These are some of the quandaries that surface for journal keepers fresh in from the fields, their baskets filled with gleanings. Sorting through and synthesizing the delicacies you have retrieved, and then naming them, can therefore spare you considerable confusion. Not only are you apt to feel more in control of your newly picked crops, but they will be more likely to deliver an abundant yield.

You can use the techniques described in this chapter as soon as you have finished rereading one journal. Those in chapter 6 lend themselves to insights gleaned from two or more journals. Of course, you may "cheat" and use any of these approaches whenever they call to you.

Unfinished Sentences

Unfinished sentences can help you reflect on and synthesize what you've harvested. Browse through the prompts below and mark those that attract you, or make up your own if you like. Pick one to begin with. Put it at the top of a blank page in your harvesting journal, label it "Harvesting My Journal from (month, date, year) to (month, date, year)," and start writing! As always, keep your hand moving to see what comes next. You may write only one line or, if the words keep pouring out, many pages. When you run dry, try another prompt. Remember, this exercise is designed to prime the pump, not guide the flow.

Complete these sentences:

What I remember most about this journal is...

I'm surprised at how often I wrote about...

I'm surprised I didn't write more about...

If I could live this period of my life over again, I would...

My greatest grief was...

My greatest joy was...

I have compassion for...

Now I can see...

I wonder why...

I am thankful...

I created...

Lists

Once you have finished rereading a journal, drawing up lists can help you organize the nuggets you've retrieved. The first exercise below will assist you in placing each nugget in a meaningful category. The second will ensure that you won't lose the good morsels you've gathered.

Compile lists using these categories, and if you like, make up some of your own:

Regrets I wrote about...

Regrets I omitted...

Places I visited...

People who played major roles in this journal...

New people I met...

Memorable moments...

Endings...

Beginnings...

If your journal seems filled with negativity, inventory the good times. Even if you didn't write about them then, you can capture them now and let your harvesting list serve as a beacon, reminding you of the light in the darkness.

Make lists based on the following topics. (Although in each instance this exercise asks you to catalog five things, list more if you like. The point is to remember the sparkling moments.)

- ◆ *Five things I like about myself during the span of time covered in this journal*
- ◆ *Five feelings, people, events, or learnings I am grateful for*
- ◆ *Five times I remember laughing*
- ◆ *Five scrumptious feasts I attended*
- ◆ *Five celebrations I want to remember*
- ◆ *Five achievements I'm proud of*
- ◆ *Five simple pleasures I enjoyed*
- ◆ *Five struggles that make me feel wiser*

Finishing Touches

Artfully arranged, the fruits of your harvest will become even more interesting. The following endeavors will help you think imaginatively and perhaps create something new from the contents of your journal.

Dedicate your journal. Rosalie, for example, dedicated one of hers to her daughter. In the front she wrote: "To Kelli-Lynne — If you read this journal, my meaning is simple. I have written to remember. May you, too, taste my life."

Think of the journal you've just harvested as a chapter in your life. Give it a title and subtitle at the top of the first page or on the cover.

Give yourself a pen name as author of this journal. Or perhaps different segments call for different noms de plume. One of Alison's journals now has segments written by Worry Wort, Dream Catcher, Dragon Slayer, She Who Copes, and Warrior Writer.

Use your senses to sum up the journal. What "color" is it? What is its "rhythm"? "Texture"? "Smell"? "Sound"? Asking questions like these gets your entire being involved — not just your head, emotions, ego, or personality, which rarely tell you anything new. Ask *all* of yourself to describe the journal and you'll discover surprising new insights.

Consider yourself a cinematographer. What images would you shoot to portray the story told in this journal? What music would you use for the sound track? Sketch out a storyboard for this production.

Dialogue with your journal to find out what it is saying to you. Ask the journal questions and listen for the answers. Here are some questions you might ask:

◆ *Before I put you aside, what do you want me to remember?*

◆ *Which of your pages feel incomplete?*

◆ *Is there anything I missed while reviewing your contents?*

◆ *What ideas do you want me to expand on in the future?*

◆ *Do you have any questions to ask me?*

Reread parts of your journal aloud. Notice when your words ring true, when you sound most like yourself. Recognize when your words sound wooden, distant, overly vague, abstract, or intellectual. Can you detect a change in the sound and rhythm of your words across this chronicle of different periods in your life? If so, what might that mean? Listening to the "music" in your words, collect the most resonant lines and turn them into a poem, a chant, or a song.

Track the verbs you used repeatedly in your journal. These "doing" words will give you an at-a-glance understanding of your accomplishments or quests. Recurring verbs can also help you spot areas of resistance or self-sabotage.

As it turned out, while we were each harvesting one of our earliest journals, we were surprised to find we shared only three recurring verbs: *celebrate, imagine,* and *invite.* Some of Alison's other frequently used verbs were *affirm, applaud, appreciate, challenge, cherish, connect, create, discover, evoke, evolve, explore, immerse, intrigue, relish, remember, reveal, slay, spiral,* and *whine.* Rosalie's other most often used verbs included *challenge, commit, consecrate, dare, desire, fascinate, free, grieve, indulge, nourish, question, recognize, search,* and *surrender.*

Imagine constructing a time capsule to represent this journal. What objects and images would you place inside it? Write a letter or make a cassette tape for those who might open it years from now. What would you most want them to know about you over the time period recorded in your journal?

Maps

Mapping techniques can help you represent your thoughts visually, making them more accessible to you than those expressed in sentences, paragraphs, or even outlines. Maps have another advantage over outlines — namely, they are not linear or hierarchical, so the order in which you record events does not matter.

MIND MAPS

Mind maps will help you quickly uncover patterns and hidden relationships between the entries in your journal. Best of all, mind mapping is so flexible that there's no way to do it wrong!

To construct a mind map of experiences and perceptions you want to remember, begin by writing the title of your journal in the center of a sheet of paper. If you haven't titled this volume, simply write the opening and closing dates of your entries. Draw a small circle around the title or dates. Now working around it in any order you like, begin capturing in short phrases the material you wish to remember. Around each item draw a circle, connecting it back to the center. To record details about any item, draw lines out from its circle and write them there. Soon these, too, may spawn circles.

Here is a mind map from one of Alison's journals to guide you as you begin:

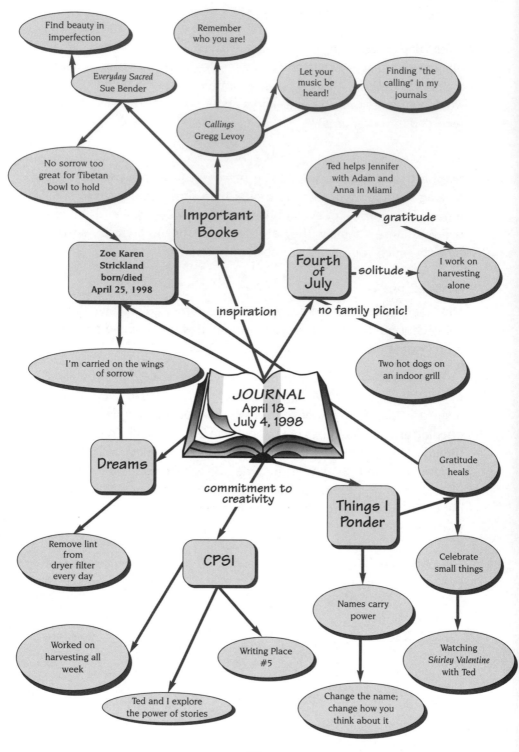

Find beauty in imperfection

Everyday Sacred
Sue Bender

Remember who you are!

Let your music be heard!

Finding "the calling" in my journals

Callings
Gregg Levoy

No sorrow too great for Tibetan bowl to hold

Ted helps Jennifer with Adam and Anna in Miami

gratitude

Important Books

Zoe Karen Strickland born/died April 25, 1998

Fourth of July

solitude

I work on harvesting alone

inspiration

no family picnic!

I'm carried on the wings of sorrow

JOURNAL
April 18 –
July 4, 1998

Two hot dogs on an indoor grill

Dreams

commitment to creativity

Things I Ponder

Gratitude heals

Remove lint from dryer filter every day

CPSI

Celebrate small things

Worked on harvesting all week

Writing Place #5

Names carry power

Watching Shirley Valentine with Ted

Ted and I explore the power of stories

Change the name; change how you think about it

After you have finished, review your map. To illustrate interrelationships you see between items that spring from the center, connect them with new lines. As your map grows, you may notice unforeseen interconnections between your thoughts. These can be color coded with highlighters.

Using your first map as a rough draft, you may want to draw a new version that groups related thoughts together and uses color coding to indicate interrelationships. You can also add symbols and sketches. Some people turn their mind maps into works of art suitable for display. Others incorporate mind mapping into their current journal keeping, stopping every now and then to quickly capture thoughts and then write from the map.

LIFE MAP

A life map is a visual history of your life that illustrates important events and turning points. You can include anything else you want to track over time. Alison, who didn't reread her journals in chronological order, wanted to track sequential periods of time and look for patterns. As she read each journal, she recorded key events on sticky notes. She then arranged them chronologically on a large piece of chart paper. That way she could read her journals in whatever order she liked and still arrive at a year-by-year record of her experiences. Some day she plans to use this record as a model for an illustrated life map, perhaps in collage form.

6

Techniques to Use with a Series of Journals

Once you have worked with several journals, try stopping to view your crops from a broader perspective. The techniques in this chapter build on earlier exercises by stimulating more connections and revealing larger patterns. Tracking your growth and transformation over long periods of time will also deepen your grasp of the wisdom you have gleaned and point the way into the future.

Feel free to work with these strategies any time you want to synthesize the material you've gathered from your journals. Begin by compiling the suggested lists to stir your memory — an activity that invites new associations. Then assemble the subsequent collections; these will encourage you to think more deeply about the transformations you have undergone. Throughout, allow memories to cross-pollinate your blossoming sense of who you are and how you "tick."

Lists for Detecting Connections and Patterns

These five listing exercises can open doors to hidden remembrances. They are best approached in the spirit of joyous excavation. Following each set of instructions are segments from our own lists to help call back your forgotten memories.

PLACES IN WHICH YOU HAVE WRITTEN

This listing exercise will awaken memories of sites where you've written. While revisiting each one, look for connections between your recorded thoughts or perceptions and the landscape or tenor of the place. Working with this list is likely to convince you of your capacity to write anywhere at any time.

Prepare a roster of places you have stopped in to write. Then conclude with a wish list for the future.

ROSALIE'S WRITING PLACES:

~ Bali, Indonesia

~ In the cellar

~ In a round chapel in Crestone, Colorado

~ At the back of a church during my daughter's wedding rehearsal

~ In a narrow hospital bed after a hysterectomy

~ Between the front paws of the sphinx in Giza, Egypt

~ At pajama parties

~ Overlooking the Gorge in Taos, New Mexico

~ In my head while having sex (never while making love)

~ At Disneyworld

I wish to write underwater.

ALISON'S WRITING PLACES:

~ In airports and on planes

~ During workshops

~ In a hospital emergency room

~ In hotel rooms

~ On beaches from Provincetown to Key West

~ In a hotel courtyard in Paris

~ At a national zoo

~ On a floating dock beside a lagoon where dolphins played

~ In doctors' waiting rooms

~ In the shade of the live oak tree beside my pool

I wish to write amid the sacred stones of Scotland.

UNDERLYING MOTIFS

Hidden beneath the primary themes expressed in your journals lie personal aspects discernible from a long-range view. As you work through this exercise, prepare for new revelations.

Complete the unfinished sentences below, adding to them all as you progress. As before, conclude with a wish list.

I've filled my journals with...

I could write entire books about...

I've become an expert in...

I'm sick of whining about...

Here's what Rosalie wrote about becoming an expert:

I've become an expert in...

~ Asking provocative questions of myself and others.

~ Linking my attitudes to the events and people I attract. (When I've been dissatisfied with external situations, I practice altering my attitudes.)

~ Acting on intuitive hunches.

~ Anticipating how much writing time I require each day so I can pass myself off as reasonably well-adjusted.

I wish to become an expert in...

~ Remembering where I put the portable phone, car keys, shopping lists, and my appointment book.

~ Expressing intimacy.

~ Polishing my writing.

~ Tantric sex.

Here's what Alison wrote about whining:

I'm sick of whining about...

~ My disorganized office.

~ Not publishing enough work.

~ Money and bag lady fears.

~ Impatience with my partner's impatience.

~ Bank accounts that don't balance, tax forms and sales reports that confound me, computers that misbehave, and swarms of pesky details that plague me.

~ Photographs that make me look older than I feel.

~ Whining.

I wish to...

~Celebrate successes, however small.

~Think about what I want instead of what I don't want.

~Write about the blessings I'm grateful for.

~Whine only for the fun of it.

BIG, BOLD LIFE-CHANGING CHOICES

The choices you have consciously made to alter an aspect of your life are worthy of recording. Why? To serve as reminders of your ability to manifest positive change the next time you feel unsure of yourself or incapable of making a good decision.

List the big, bold choices you have documented that you knew would change your life. Reviewing this list will help build courage.

ALISON'S LIST:

~To return to graduate school

~To claim my creativity

~To "break rank" and follow my own woman's path

~To divorce

~To leave my secure position with a school system to start my own business

~To marry my business partner

~To confront my dragons one by one

~To spend more than a year writing with almost no income

~To hold my tiny newborn granddaughter as she died

ROSALIE'S LIST:

~To reinvest in life despite the death of my teenage son

~To honor the voice of my intuition

~To tell the truth in my family

~To protect my daughter regardless of the cost

~To move to New Mexico to begin a life in the mountains

~To surrender to my vulnerability

~ To claim my power

~ To trust myself to risk intimacy once again

~ To give up being nice for being knowing

~ To decide to give up working for writing and experiencing

~ To begin my own publishing company

~ To honor my connection with spirit daily

SEEMINGLY INSIGNIFICANT CHOICES

Seemingly insignificant choices take time to reveal their impact, yet they often turn out to have the most profound outcomes. Tracking these decisions will remind you that life often unfolds in unexpected ways and that the smallest choices can make enormous differences.

Jot down the mundane choices you've recorded that ultimately changed the course of your life. Perhaps a chance phone call to an acquaintance led to a perfect job, or maybe you accepted a casual invitation and met your true love.

Alison's son, for example, met his wife, Beth, at a party both of them considered not attending. They left the affair together, and that's where they've been ever since. As soon as she met Beth, Alison wrote in her journal, "Jason has met his soul mate. He may not know it yet, but Beth is the woman he's going to marry."

TRUTHS

Plucking out truth blossoms from your journals can help you trace the voice of your authentic self. In the process you will find truths that have changed over time and others that remain constant.

Keep an ongoing list of your expressed truths. Toward this end, be sure to reserve plenty of blank "truth" pages in a special notebook or a separate file on your computer, because your truth crop will grow with each journal you review.

ROSALIE'S TRUTHS:

~ Birds are the last creatures to leave the forest during a fire.

~ I remain connected to good friends even after a move.

∿I have tried to understand my emotions with my head.

∿I suffer when I do not express my creativity.

∿Mothering is one of my biggest life lessons.

ALISON'S TRUTHS:

∿I find joy in simple things.

∿I grow more in hard times than easy ones, but I still love the easy ones!

∿There's little that popcorn can't soothe.

∿I trust intuition over intellect AND I still check things out with my intellect.

∿The sorrows of my children are harder to bear than my own.

Collections to Reflect On

These exercises encourage you to move beyond simple listing into deeper reflection. In each case, write as little or as much as you wish about the topic under investigation.

CHANGES OBSERVED OVER TIME

Returning to your early perceptions of people, places, and ideas and then noting the ways in which these have changed over the years will help you see how you have ripened. Here are two exercises that are likely to prove enlightening.

The "Good"

Changes in perception can become remarkably clear after tracking the various attributes you have ascribed to worthy aspects of your life.

Take note of your various definitions of "good" over time. Consider how your sense of each item listed below has evolved. Pick your favorites and reflect on the shifts you have made.

◆ *Good friends*   ◆ *Good actions*   ◆ *Good days*

◆ *Good times*   ◆ *Good food*   ◆ *Good beginnings*

◆ *Good parents*   ◆ *Good healers*   ◆ *Good endings*

◆ *Good teachers*   ◆ *Good luck*   ◆ *Good entertainment*

◆ *Good women*   ◆ *Good books*   ◆ *Good insights*

◆ *Good men*   ◆ *Good dreams*   ◆ *Good good-byes*

◆ *Good ideas*   ◆ *Good nights*   ◆ *Good jokes*

"I *used to*...; *now* I..."

Here is another eye-opening way to capture the changes you have noticed in yourself after reading a series of journals. Play with this exercise to your heart's content.

Consider the unfinished sentence "I used to...; now I..." Collect examples from your journals to fill in the blanks. Then let each item in your collection become an impetus for more writing. Better yet, compose an entire narrative about how you've changed.

ALISON'S COLLECTION:

∿I used to run away from unfamiliar situations; now I walk toward them.

∿I used to react; now I respond.

∿I used to believe creativity was something lucky people were born with; now I know it's a birthright.

∿I used to DEFINE myself in relationships; now I EXPRESS myself in them.

∿I used to believe that with the right partner, the right job, and the right possessions (house, car, clothes, and so on) I could find security; now I know that when I feel secure, I can manifest everything I need.

∿I used to bury pain; now I know how to name it and use it to grow stronger.

ROSALIE'S COLLECTION:

∿I used to wait until flowers were almost dead before buying another bouquet; now I visit a florist twice a week regardless of the state my flowers are in.

∿ I used to write alone; now I form writing groups wherever I happen to be.

∿ I used to pride myself on being detached in primary relationships; now I appreciate that intimacy is not a four-letter word.

∿ I used to hide my power; now I express myself and welcome the receptivity of people who are privy to my feelings and ideas.

∿ I used to judge the business world; now I am president of two companies.

∿ I used to avoid being with people who were dying; now I sit with dying friends, fully aware that my presence is enough.

LESSONS LEARNED OVER TIME

Learnings that remain valid over many years eventually evolve into wisdom. Collecting these pearls of wisdom can enhance your understanding of the insights that guide you.

To quickly find out the lessons you've learned over time, return to your list of truths, as described on page 59, and look for deeper meanings.

ROSALIE'S LEARNINGS:

∿ Because emotional integrity is as important to me as harmony and fresh air, I must be emotionally honest with myself.

∿ I am responsible for creating harmony within myself.

∿ I don't have to understand everything.

ALISON'S LEARNINGS:

∿ The longer I live, the less concerned I am with material "stuff."

∿ There's nothing like a few tragic blows to clarify what really matters.

∿ Trust only the simplicity found on the other side of complexity.

PLEASURES

Savoring your pleasures can brighten your life and nourish your soul. Even simple pleasures can work magic, such as walking in the rain, listening to a new type of music, surrendering to a nap in the middle of the day, or melting into tenderness.

Bring together the loves you have recorded in your journals. To use this collection as an ongoing source of renewal, be sure to keep it current.

The following collection sprouted from an entry Alison came upon in one of her 1994 journals. Ever since its inception she has found it fun to build upon and soothing to read.

Sam Keen, in a piece he contributed to an anthology entitled Sacred Stories, *writes about his deep need for continuity in a world that does its best to destroy any sense of continuity in our lives. Here's how he holds on to his story: "I have come to know that in this lifetime there will never be a time when I don't love peanut butter."*

What will I always love? Popcorn!

Later additions:

∾ In this lifetime I will always love watching water — ocean, gulf, puddle, fountain, creek, waterfall, rivers, lakes, ponds, raindrops. And clear water in a crystal vase filled with flowers.

∾ In this lifetime I will always love flowers — fresh daisies, big star lilies, chrysanthemums in the fall, poinsettias welcoming Christmas, and daffodils announcing spring.

∾ In this lifetime I will always love candles and Christmas trees, the scent of pine, music, the sound of rain on the roof at night, and Ted's arms around me any time.

NEW TRAITS THAT COULD BE DANGEROUS

Dangerous? Yes! As we grow into authentically expressing who we are, we often reevaluate how we want to experience and express ourselves. In the process, we let go of old patterns and experiment with new ways of being. Consequently, midway through the harvesting process, you may begin to sense portions of yourself falling away and new parts ripening.

Collect perilously unfamiliar parts of yourself that seem to be emerging. Using your intuition, explain why they may have appeared.

At this point in Rosalie's harvesting process, some of her friends remarked that she seemed dangerous. When they asked why she was breaking so many of her long-held rules, she gave them this entry:

I am a dangerous woman to be around because I am now committed to writing and speaking my truth as I know it, see it, and feel it.

I am a dangerous woman to be around because, increasingly, I respond to life passionately or not at all.

I am a dangerous woman to be around because I am dedicated to making decisions that are in alignment with my soul. I will, in turn, invite YOU to be more conscious of making purposeful choices in YOUR life.

I am a dangerous woman to be around because I will seize the opportunity to speak of my passion for the written word. And I will invite you to speak about your passions as well.

I am a dangerous woman to be around because I grow impatient listening to stories of suffering and woe. I believe we are responsible for transforming our reality if it is not in alignment with our deepest purpose. And I don't mind saying so!

I am a dangerous woman to be around because I know the planet is counting on each of us to breathe in our essence. I yearn for community with others who have consecrated their lives to their souls' evolution.

RESPONSES TO OTHERS' INSIGHTS

Words from other writers may pollinate new connections and offer a fresh vantage point from which to view your own experiences. It is a good idea to regard your responses as signs of personal growth emerging from the cuttings of another plant. As you read the following selections, imagine how you might respond to the same prompts.

ONE OF ROSALIE'S MEANINGFUL QUOTES AND HER RESPONSE TO IT:

"I had hoped to find a straight path.... Instead the path led in circles."
— Sue Bender

Straight lines and shortcuts shaped my early adult years, although I intuitively understood sacred geometry — made up, as it is, of straight lines AND circles. The more I reflect on my recent life, however, the more I appreciate curved consciousness. I see it as a realm where creator and creation coexist, where spirals merge within spirals to become circles. Sarah's dance, a circle, is about feminine consciousness. Jacob's ladder, a hierarchy, is often cited as an example of masculine consciousness. I'll take a circle any day, because when I am within a hoop I understand circumference!

ONE OF ALISON'S MEANINGFUL QUOTES AND HER RESPONSE TO IT:

"Despair, when not the response to absolute physical and moral defeat, is, like war, the failure of imagination." — Adrienne Rich

This quote is my touchstone. I keep it in my seed journal and in the notebook I carry in my purse. I found Adrienne's words just when I needed them most — as Ted lay in the hospital dazed and depressed by sudden illness. We both sensed the need to imagine a different life and a brighter outcome than our fears had allowed for, and Adrienne challenged us to do that. Several other quotes about the tragic loss of imagination came to me over the next few days, each jumping off the page. Synchronicity in action — which always appeals to my imagination!

Pick one of the following quotations and start writing, drawing on the observations you have made of your own growth and transformation:

"I wish I could convince people out there making art and writing books, that if you don't start with your own life, you're cheating." — Allie Light

"What will there be in the bad times? There will be singing about the bad times."
— Bertolt Brecht

"As I look back on what I have written, I can see that the very persons who have taken away my time are those who have given me something to say."

— Katherine Peterson

"Pay attention to what they tell you to forget."

— Muriel Ruckeyser

"One of the disciplines of building a rich soul life seems to be the simple act, on a daily basis, of remembering what is most important to us."

— David Whyte

"A woman may write her whole life in advance of living it."

— Carolyn Heilbrun

"Take care of your gift."

— Danny Glover, quoting his acting teacher Jean Shelton

Integrating Your Discoveries

What have you learned about who you were, who you are, and who you have always been? To take your discoveries even further, write out imaginative responses to each of these hypothetical situations.

Suppose that you are asked to talk about your harvesting experiences with a famous interviewer such as Bill Moyers, Oprah Winfrey, or a National Public Radio host. Write the questions you would like this person to ask you. Now enter into conversation with the interviewer, answering their questions. Dialogue with them to further explore your answers. Write up the conversation as though it were a magazine or newspaper interview.

Consider yourself a biographer — an intelligent, compassionate, insightful writer who is researching your life using your journals as a primary source. Outline the chapters. Compose the preface and the afterword. Write the jacket blurb summarizing the contents of the book. Write the entire volume if you wish!

PART III

Bundling the Sheaves

Combining Related Themes

By now, you no doubt have a good idea of the motifs that have been affecting you on either a conscious or an unconscious level. Bundling together the strands of these themes can give you a sense of your cycles and an expanded perspective on your life. While working with each one, imagine that you carry a high-power telescope in one hand and a high-power microscope in the other — one to help you spot the big picture and the other to zoom in on the tiny pieces.

The following chapters contain bundles from our harvest. After each one are our responses to the reflective writing exercise described on pages 41–42, together with an invitation to write. Your replies are likely to spark new thoughts about your own bundles and perhaps even the emergence of a "volunteer" theme or two.

7

Miss Perfect

From Alison's Journals

Struggles with my perfectionist streak appear in all my journals. Batching together some entries about the perils of perfectionism (there were far too many to include them all!) has helped me catch myself whenever I stumble into that old trap, and has inspired me to make peace with Miss Perfect.

SEPTEMBER 7, 1989

For years I've taught people how to give positive feedback first and then turn critical thoughts into solution-oriented statements, such as "How might we...," instead of "Why don't you...," or worse, "Why didn't you..." Only recently have I realized that the person I most often forget to do this with is ME.

My addiction to perfection makes it harder for me to experiment. My need to be an expert at everything I do keeps me from "beginner's mind." Both these forces pose barriers to creativity. Actually, I want to be an expert at TRYING NEW THINGS! I want to excel in cutting myself some slack.

Nurturing parent and playful child make good partners for this project. Together, we go out stalking dragons, cutting ropes so prisoners can escape, blowing fog away from swamps where dragons lurk. We befriend dragons, sing lullabies, tell funny stories, invent new dances, draw on sidewalks, and lick ice cream cones. Together, we can set the creative spirit free once more.

SEPTEMBER 1, 1990 (JENNIFER'S WEDDING DAY)

Of course, I want everything to be perfect on my daughter's special day.

There is within me a 'fraidy cat and a tyrant of a perfectionist. They block creative accomplishment. They also steal pleasure. I vow to leave them both at home today!

FEBRUARY 1, 1991

A decade ago, at just this time of year, I learned something I've never forgotten — something that might help to ward off Miss Perfect. At an early morning workshop during The Whole Brain Symposium in Key West, Bob, our group leader, helped us explore ways to stay centered. When we gathered on the beach shortly after sunrise, he asked us to form a circle and practice following our breath and focusing attention on our centers until we felt solidly present standing there on the sand. Then he walked behind us, gently pushing against our backs. If we didn't wobble, we'd successfully found our centers and grounded ourselves. I loved how calm and peaceful I felt watching the water and listening to the waves lap onto shore, my bare feet planted firmly on the earth. When Bob pushed against my back, I didn't move.

Next, he went to the center of the circle and tossed a battered old rubber flip-flop onto the sand. He asked us to look at this sandal and think about all the things we disliked about it. I called up my annoyance with people who litter beaches, who spoil natural settings by carelessly discarding their garbage. This time as Bob pushed gently against my back, I nearly toppled over. Busy finding fault with the flip-flop, I hadn't noticed his approach. Clearly, I'd lost touch with my center, lost my awareness, and lost the peaceful feelings I'd enjoyed earlier.

Bob then invited us to look at the flip-flop with appreciation and heartfelt regard for its service. I remembered beautiful days on the beach when similar sandals kept shells from cutting into my feet. I thought about how good it felt to kick off high-heeled shoes and put on sandals. I recalled the tiny ones I'd bought for my children when they were little. At that point the old flip-flop symbolized freedom, seaside vacations, peaceful walks on the beach, children playing in the sand. When Bob once again pushed against my back, I did not move. *FOCUS ON FLAWS AND I LOSE MY CENTER; LOOK WITH APPRECIATION AND I'M GROUNDED AND CONTENT.*

When Miss Perfect arrives with her judgments, I lose my center, just as I did that day. I think I'll talk to her about it. She likes to know I learn my lessons well.

JANUARY 24, 1992 (AFTER A TWO-WEEK BOUT OF THE FLU)

Reading an interview with Julia Cameron exhausted me. She talks about life as pure creative energy that infuses us all. Well, where is it? Today I'm feeling just well enough to get REALLY frustrated with my low productivity on the creative front and REALLY annoyed with her. Instead of motivating me, she tires me out!

Miss Perfect pipes up with: "If you were creative and talented, if you were at all special or gifted, you'd work despite illness and discouragement. You'd quickly recover from the virus that lays others low for weeks. With willpower and dedication, you'd rise above your fatigue and sniffing and coughing, and write a terrific article. You're just a lightweight who can't cope."

What is this incessant sabotage from the perfectionist? Why can't I just let myself be, and place no demands beyond loving and caring for ME? Have I ever done that? I don't think so.

SEPTEMBER 10, 1992

A found quote from Anaïs Nin: "There are very few human beings who receive the truth, complete and staggering by instant illumination. Most of them acquire it fragment by fragment on a small scale, by successive developments cellularly, like a laborious mosaic."

I must remind myself of the laborious mosaic. It's a powerful metaphor. Miss Perfect expects me to be clear and profound every time I pick up my pen. She can't understand why I haven't published numerous books by now. "How many years is it going to take you to figure all this out?" she asks irritably, hands on hips, foot tapping impatiently.

Well, I guess the rest of my life, and that's not just OK — it's perfect!

APRIL 20, 1994

This morning I found these lines from Angeles Arrien's *Four-Fold Way* that speak directly to one of my biggest life lessons: "Believing you can be perfect is the fatal imperfection. Believing you're invulnerable is the ultimate vulnerability. Being a Warrior doesn't mean winning or even succeeding. It means risking and failing and risking again, as long as you live."

What a great shield this is against sneak attacks from Miss Perfect! I don't think I ever believed I COULD be perfect, but I certainly thought I SHOULD be. Miss Perfect wants to keep control at all times, so this quote tells me she wants to be invulnerable. And in spite of all that, I've taken big risks in my life. In the clear moments I know that what matters is showing up, staying present, getting up when I stumble, going on, saying YES! That's what warriors do.

JUNE 29, 1994

Ted and I have come to Lido Beach for our annual corporate "advance" — a few days to relax, walk the beach, and think about where we've been and where we wish to go. Sitting alone here on the deck gazing at the blue gulf waters, I realize Miss Perfect's come along. She's complaining about the things I forgot to bring. She's pissed off because I forgot my hat and suntan lotion and will have to pay tourist prices for them on St. Armand's Key in the morning.

Miss Perfect, you are such a pain in the ass! Leave me to the whisper of the palm fronds and the squawks of the gulls. Let me mesmerize myself by watching sea oats sway in the wind, sunlight turning their tips golden. Let my peaceful, even breathing blow you away. You've been with me since I was a little girl, when I thought if I could just be good enough I wouldn't die. Well, fifty years is too long! Your lease is up. We need to find you a better place to hang out.

A gull lands on the piling in front of me, and I begin to sketch it. As I draw, it occurs to me that I must treat Miss Perfect with compassion. She so wants everything to be just right and doesn't understand that it already is when I see clearly instead of distorting things, finding them flawed and in need of fixing. I begin sketching sea oats and defy her to find fault with my efforts. All I hear is the wind.

NOVEMBER 19, 1996 (WHILE TEACHING IN NORTH CAROLINA)

Today, while walking the hills as Ted worked with the group, I listened to one of Carolyn Myss's *Energy Anatomy* tapes. "How honest are you with yourself? How truthful?" she asks her audience. I immediately began searching for ways I deceive myself. Do I really want to write? Do I struggle because I've neither the talent nor will required to be an excellent writer? Do I deceive myself with foolish daydreams and impractical, wishful new age fuzzy beliefs? What happened to the sharp existential edge I honed right here in North Carolina as a literature major studying male writers and male critics?

All this ruminating took only took a couple of moments before Carolyn nailed me. She explained that upon hearing the question of honesty, people tend to get critical of themselves. Rarely do they say, "Well, I'm really *good* at... and I'm a *talented....,*" or "I was born to...." Those are the truths we must tell ourselves.

So sitting here by the lake at sunset, journal in my lap, I say I'm a born teacher. I'm also a born reader; and if I'd had a teacher like me, I'd have known much earlier that I'm a fine writer as well. I'm good at seeing the larger perspective and synthesizing ideas. I see patterns across disciplines. I'm a skilled facilitator. I can command attention and fill up a room. I can make complex ideas understandable. I know how to create an atmosphere where people feel comfortable enough to risk, learn, create. I invent lots of interesting ways to make key points when I teach. And I don't have to do it all perfectly!

JUNE 25, 1997

A note from Kay: "The difference between perfectionism and going for excellence is this. PERFECTIONISM is fear based and needy — a desire to please, to be accepted, but feeling unworthy. GOING FOR EXCELLENCE is love based — a willingness to inspire and be inspired by going the distance, including the details and fine-tuning."

Rereading Kay's wise words, I appreciate the recurring tension between fear and love. May my striving for excellence always springs from love — love of both the work and the purpose it fulfills. Perhaps I should grant Miss Perfect more love and appreciation rather than try to drive her out.

OCTOBER 6, 1997

"Stop trying to 'fix' things, especially yourself. You're already enough — more than enough." Good advice to myself that I found while rereading my journals.

IN TALKING WITH OTHER WRITERS:

"Sin is the failure to grow."
— Gregory of Nyssa, fourth-century theologian

Sin, when I was little, meant not being perfect, making a mistake, screwing up. It took me a long time to learn that screwing up was a wonderful learning strategy IF you can let go of blame and judgment, replacing them with curiosity and flexibility. Curiosity is the best antidote against getting stuck in blame and judgment. I think I need to talk with Miss Perfect about curiosity. I suspect she still believes it killed the cat.

"To realize originality one has to have the courage to be an amateur."
— Marianne Moore, poet

Well, Miss Perfect frowns upon amateurism. Perhaps I should have her arrested for murdering creativity!

"Be loving and lighthearted in all your activities."
I don't know where I got this quote, but I think it's impossible to do. Perhaps the loving part is possible, at least for saints; but lighthearted isn't. Sometimes things go wrong. Sometimes the world breaks your heart. If Miss Perfect got hold of this one, she'd bitch at me when I wake up tired and grumpy. Better toss it!

"Treating myself like a precious object will make me strong."
— found on the inside front cover of a journal

Too often I catch myself in an act of self-abuse. When I was growing up, self-abuse meant masturbation. Would that it were the only form I ever practiced!

JUNE 5, 1998 (AFTER READING SUE BENDER'S *Everyday Sacred*)

"Don't try for perfection... trying for good enough will be plenty."
I should put this one up on my refrigerator door, right beside my grandchildren's "good enough" drawings!

"The Latin root of the word PERFECT means only 'finished,' not 'without flaws.'" A woman who'd spent years living and writing about the Shakers sent Sue this quote. She included it in her book, in a section about purposefully cracking pots, firing the pieces, then gluing them back together to form a vessel much more artful than an unmarred one. The metaphor's rich.

After Sue finished putting her broken bowl back together, she said: "This bowl looks far more interesting, more beautiful than before it broke. The pieces are the same, but it's a different bowl than when I started." Yes, perfection can be boring! It may even lead to decay, for it leaves nothing behind to encourage new growth.

At the close of *Everyday Sacred*, Sue refers to a series of imperfect Zen tea bowls she had made, explaining: "Most of us are like those Zen tea bowls — uneven, cracked, imperfect. And our harsh judge keeps wishing we were perfect. The difference is the tea bowls are revered JUST AS THEY ARE. Our imperfections are a gift, the very qualities that make us unique. If we make the shift to see them that way, we can value ourselves as the monks valued those tea bowls, JUST AS WE ARE."

From now on I will keep the imperfect tea bowls in mind as I reread my journals. "Harsh judge" sounds a lot scarier than Miss Perfect, who's so much easier to befriend. It feels like we are at last reaching a truce.

Reflective Writing:

∿ I LEARNED that I don't have to be perfect to be good. I found the roots of Miss Perfect in my primary education and in my determination to be such a good girl that I wouldn't die like my sister. My "excellent" elementary school education taught me not to trust myself. My religious education in the Protestant church stifled my spirit. Both environments had me afraid of making mistakes.

∿ I RELEARNED that I never got far trying to battle Miss Perfect.

∿ I DISCOVERED that to tame her, befriend her, and get her on my side, I had to honor her good intentions and assign her specific duties.

～**I REDISCOVERED** that at times I also had to tell her when to leave me alone.

～**I REGRET** that she kept me from putting my work out into the world.

～**I APPRECIATE** that she wanted to serve me well by prodding me to do my best.

～**RIGHT NOW I FEEL** amused by her and confident in myself.

～**AND I WILL** be sure to let her know when she's being a pain in the ass. (She just told me to rephrase "pain in the ass." I overruled her.)

Invitation to Write

Is there a part of *you* that craves perfection? If so, how does that part get in your way? How does it serve you? If you are among the lucky ones who don't suffer from perfectionism, how did you escape the curse? What would you say to those who are not so fortunate?

8

Dreams

*F*ROM ROSALIE'S JOURNALS

Dreams remind me of plants growing in a shady corner of my garden, or underground; sometimes they even warn me of dangerous circumstances. Appreciating the value of my unconscious long ago propelled me to keep a separate dream journal and to have a friend as a "dream buddy." A stirring dream I had more recently ushered me into a twelve-month exploration of my dreams with a "dream guide."

Here are a series of dreams culled from my dream journal, bundled chronologically, and titled. Following the first dream are suggestions for working with those of your own. The succeeding entries incorporate these suggestions, illustrating ways that you, too, can gain clarity from dreams. At the end of the chapter, you will find, as before, an example of reflective writing and an invitation to write, complete with quotations to spur you on.

(1985) Essence

I am walking down Main Street in my hometown carrying a small glass oil-lamp in a plain paper bag. The bag slips from my hand and shatters against the concrete pavement. I watch as oil seeps into the ground. I am upset because I had filled the lamp with two ounces of white rose essence. I console myself by remembering that I have two vials of lotus essence left, although only one of white rose.

I remind myself that I can buy more essence when I return to Egypt. Then I surprise myself by acknowledging that my essence is not outside me, and is surely not contained in an oil lamp. Walking on, I giggle at this realization, yet I consciously resist sharing my joy with strangers I meet. For the moment, it is enough for ME to know the reason for my glee.

You could take the same steps I do to gain clarity from a dream:

◆ *Name the dream.*
◆ *Write it in the present tense as if it were happening now.*
◆ *Highlight the significant verbs.* This helps me track the movement of the dream, letting me know if it is moving forward, stuck in time, or going in reverse.
◆ *Underline intriguing words, phrases, or sentences, and intuit their meanings.* For example, <u>white rose essence</u> is my most cherished fragrance; I'd bought it in Egypt six years before. When I relax and ask for the deeper meaning of this phrase, I am aware that white rose is associated with my spirituality. I am perplexed about the statement "<u>I can buy more essence.</u>" Is "buying" the same as "investing in"? When <u>I giggle</u>, I relax into a soft awareness. Too much serious questioning causes me to lose track of what I know about the laws of mirth. Because I tend to share insights as they occur to me, I am fascinated by the sentence "<u>For the moment, it is enough for *me* to know...</u>" Yet I remember that at the start of each of my pregnancies I embraced the precious news in solitude for a while.
◆ *List the polarities.* While noting these opposing qualities, I ask myself if they seem to be playing out their struggle in my life as well. The polarities in this dream include concrete–essence and upset–giggle.
◆ *Listen to what the dream is saying, and write it out in a few paragraphs of initial reflections.* "Essence," I believe, is reminding me to acknowledge my inner core and embrace it joyfully. Being content to keep this new knowledge to myself feels right.
◆ *Take action on the dream.* I will dab some white rose essence behind my ears and enjoy breathing in my spirituality, even if I do have only two ounces left.

(1991) The Surprise Offering

I AM STANDING at the door of a crowded college classroom. <u>I FEEL vulnerable and excited</u>. I TAKE a deep breath and ANNOUNCE to the students that I NO LONGER HAVE PASSION FOR THE COURSE I AGREED to teach. They LOOK disappointed. Then I DECLARE, "I PLAN to teach something new."

A student ASKS me the name of the course. "I DO NOT HAVE a title for it," I REPLY, "because I HAVE NOT FORMULATED its content in my mind."

I then ASK the students if they WISH to remain in my class. I am amazed that everyone ELECTS to stay in a course that is still under development.

Initial Reflections:

This dream feels like windows to my soul. Rather than formulating anything, I am trusting in an intangible process that is evolving within me. My passion is alive in each moment, which is a challenge for the part of me that prides itself on being responsible. I feel ready for the unexpected, and much to my surprise I am received!

Polarities include student–teacher and excited–disappointed.

Yes, I can be received just as I am, no matter how formless or undefined my thoughts may be. I will resist all temptations to impose my will and take charge of this situation.

(1992) The Future

I AM TAKING a qualifying exam in a different state. Initially, the exam LOOKS like a standard IQ test, except that all the questions are about science: measurement of light and density, absorption rates, and locations of stellar beams.

As I READ the questions, I SUSPECT I have the wrong exam. The proctor INFORMS me that everyone has to pass the exam in order to PRACTICE their specialty. Glancing around the room filled with men, I DISCOVER that everyone but me looks like a scientist.

"There must be some way around this," I WHISPER to myself. Then looking at the wall, I NOTICE a calendar marked March 7, 2007. Suddenly, I REALIZE that everybody in the room shares a similar background in healing. I UNDERSTAND immediately that all healers HAVE TO BE EDUCATED in the new sciences and that all scientists HAVE TO BE EDUCATED in healing.

I especially LIKE the practical part of the exam, because it REQUIRES me to demonstrate my out-of-body expertise. While checking the coordinates, factoring in density and absorption rates, and assuming the positions of the stellar beams, I BEGIN FLYING to my home state of Maine, thinking, "I'm <u>en route to Me.</u>" I LIKE <u>the spirit of this out-of-body adventure</u> and start SHOWING OFF by practicing advanced acrobatics, unaware that this, too, is part of the qualifying exam.

Initial Reflections:

The phrase "en route to Me." reminds me that I am coming home to myself in a new way. What leads is no longer my mind but rather the spirit of out-of-body adventures.

Polarities include me—men, healers—scientists, and practical—out of body.

This dream is asking me to acknowledge myself as both a healer and a student of science. As such, I welcome in the energy of the future, breathe into it, and ask it to converse with me.

ME: Welcome, Future. I'm curious about your role in my dream and in my life. Please communicate with me.

FUTURE: Thanks for the invitation. I am forever in contact with you. Sometimes you dismiss me, yet at other times you listen to my whispers.

ME: You're right. You remind me of the Rainer Maria Rilke quotation I have on the inside cover of one of my journals, which says, "The future enters into us in order to transform us long before the event."

FUTURE: That's an accurate job description — not too long-winded or filled with platitudes.

ME: I sense you are connected to my healing practice. What do I need to know?

FUTURE: Without science, you limit your education and your ability to understand and implement principles of physics. You have created a division in your consciousness. Embracing the future of science is part of your healing.

ME: Okay, I rejected the sciences when I was in college; poetry and literature were more interesting. Yet I enjoy listening to engineer and scientist friends.

FUTURE: Think of science as part of your shadow, an unintegrated piece of your potential. It is not too late — remember, the calendar said 2007.

ME: Thank you. I promise to prepare now for the future.

(Note: In June 1997 I met a scientist who works at NASA. The following September I joined ten other people at a five-day conference on healing in space. The first night, we shared our reasons for attending the conference, whereupon I read my dream. Nobody laughed. I felt comfortable and ready to learn.)

(1994) The Kiss

I AM SITTING on the worn green couch in my parents' living room. My entire family is present, and my younger brother INTRODUCES a friend. I am bored. My brother's friend, who SEEMS TO INTUIT that I AM NOT INTERESTED in the conversation, asks me if I want to try something different.

Without questioning what he has in mind, I REPLY, "Of course."

He PULLS me toward him and KISSES my lips!

I ENJOY his kiss, which feels more playful than sexual. The conversation around us STOPS. Everyone LOOKS shocked. I SMILE and SAY nothing.

The scene shifts to a small room, where I am SITTING with my father, brother, ex-husband, and a priest. Each of them LECTURES me about my unconventional behavior. I DO NOT UNDERSTAND why they are so concerned, but I sense it IS CONNECTED with the kiss.

My father, a traditional man, FACES me and says sternly, "We are deeply worried about you." Everybody nods. To me, the kiss is simply a spontaneous gesture. In fact, I had not thought of it since it happened.

My father CONTINUES, "If you do not give up your unconventional ways, you will no longer be a member of this family."

I AM AMAZED that everyone has taken the kiss so seriously. As for me, I HAD ALREADY CHOSEN TO BE AVAILABLE for unexpected times of magic and awakening. I SIGH, get up from my chair, STAND in front of each man, and leaning over, KISS him on the cheek. Then without speaking, I WALK out. As I GREET the fresh air, I PRAY that someday they, too, might APPRECIATE the meaning of the kiss.

Initial Reflections:

I feel honest having acknowledged my reality, even though it differs from that of my family. Conventional thinking and behavior bore me. Considering that all the others in this dream are men, I wonder if it is the traditional masculine that I am moving away from — in favor of the more spontaneous masculine embodied by my brother's friend. What does this dream reflect about my inner masculine that holds tradition and family values as sacred? I appreciate the receptivity and assertiveness I demonstrated, yet it was my growing sense of mischief and daring that served as a launchpad for announcing myself to the men in my family.

Polarities include family–friend, traditional–unconventional, and lecture–kiss.

The sweetness and innocence of the kiss reminds me to be present for the unexpected. I will continue to explore the edges of my psyche by honoring the truth of my own experiences.

(1995) Desperate Search

I am at the beach with a three-year-old child. <u>I am nervous, because I am in charge of his safety and he is a daredevil</u>. Without warning, he DARTS for the ocean and SWIMS out into deep water. I take off after him, but he DIVES underwater and DOES NOT COME UP. I PANIC! Several people JOIN in the rescue mission. <u>We dive deep down to reach him, but he SEEMS TO HAVE DISAPPEARED</u>. All I can think of is the broad smile that covered his sweet little face while he was at play on the beach.

Initial Reflections:

The action here seems fast and abrupt, leaving me with little time to breathe. It is as though something bigger is trying to happen and I, the dreamer, am stuck in a narrow role. I want to understand, and I know that means diving deeply into areas I have never before explored. The reversal in this dream fascinates me: I am the guardian and a three year old is the daredevil. "In what ways is this child my teacher?" I ask myself.

Polarities include adult–child, panic–smile, and rescue–play.

Believing we are all that we dream, I intentionally merge my energies with those of the characters in an effort to give them their voices and discover their values.

ADULT IN CHARGE: I am the protector, guardian of the child. I know best what is good for him.

THREE YEAR OLD: I am spontaneity, the creative impulse that plunges in and dives deep. I coexist with eternity; I wish to play with the adults and remind them of dimensions they have denied or forgotten. I do not understand why they fear for me, especially when I am free.

OTHER ADULTS: We need to save this child from himself. He is in water over his head and will drown. Rescuing him is all that matters. Why didn't she watch him more closely? He never should have gotten ahead of her.

OCEAN: My depths are available. Transformation awaits. The child is my emissary. What you imagine as life is death; what you imagine as drowning is living.

I feel optimistic rather than upset. I desire to live from my soul. I invite transformation, knowing I am not in control. Yet sometimes my "responsible adult" takes over and acts as if physical reality is all that matters. I appreciate that my inner child is a daredevil leading the way. Still, I miss my son Mike although he died eighteen years ago. The sweet smile on the child's face was HIS.

(1995) The Dream Call

I AM SITTING in a rocking chair sipping tea in my kitchen. The large, round room has seven huge windows and looking through them I AM FASCINATED by the play of light on the nearby mountaintop. I feel content.

Noises from the living room DISTURB me. I WALK into the sunlit room just in time to see a young boy scramble behind my favorite brown leather lounge chair. I ORDER him to come out. He looks about eight years old and is wearing loose dungarees, a sweatshirt, and a baseball cap askew on top of his head. Sneakers HIDE his feet. I KNOW by looking at him that he is a "scrapper."

"What are you doing in my house?" I DEMAND to know in a loud voice of authority.

He RAISES his chin and LOOKS me in the eye. "Visiting," he replies.

"How can you be visiting when you WERE NEVER INVITED?"

"I COME here often. This is the first time you've CAUGHT me, though."

I DO NOT KNOW what to say, other than TO SCREAM, "You have no right to be here without an invitation. You BROKE INTO my house."

"Look, lady, I've never STOLEN anything. You've never even KNOWN I was here. Besides, <u>I DON'T NEED your invitation; I'll come whenever I like.</u>"

"Says who?" I challenged.

"Says me."

"You have no right to barge in on my privacy!" I SCREAM.

I REACH out and GRAB his shirt. He SCOOTS to the right. Stepping closer to him, I grab his arms, and without warning we TOPPLE to the floor, POUNDING and KICKING each other. He HITS my cheek with his fist; I LAND a slap on his rump. As he SQUIRMS away, I POUNCE on him again.

We WRESTLE until we are exhausted. <u>I am astounded that I have been out of control</u> with an eight-year-old kid, belligerent though he may be. Out of breath, we each MOVE AWAY. <u>I STRUGGLE to be my grown-up self</u> once more as he WATCHES me intensely.

"Okay, kid, I UNDERSTAND you like it here. <u>I also OWN this home, and I am in charge.</u> How about if we agree that I WILL INVITE you here for cocoa and cookies, and you WON'T COME until asked?"

He shrugs his small shoulders, pulls up his droopy pants, and SWAGGERS to the door, baseball cap tilted to the left. While waving good-bye, he says, "<u>Lady, you can invite me if you want, but I'll come back whenever I feel like it.</u>"

Initial Reflections:

I awoke from the dream feeling exasperated and judgmental toward myself. Why? Because my passion for privacy felt primal, and because I had been a terrible bully. On another level, I admit that it is time to explore the masculine part of myself, since I do not wish to attract a scrappy eight year old for a partner.

Polarities include adult woman–eight-year-old boy, contentment–anger, invitation–invasion, reason–emotion, control–loss of control, and right–left.

Perhaps I ought to give myself credit, as my inner child has grown from a three-year-old daredevil to an eight-year-old rebel. In any case, this is a breakthrough dream, and I am ready to grow myself up!

(1995) Integration

I am an actress on a movie set. The male director sits about six feet off the ground in a director's chair. I AM WEARING a soft pink dress that is almost transparent when the sunlight hits it from behind. I prepare to WALK toward a man who is about eight feet in front of me — and naked. I AM AWARE of his beauty as well as my own. I DO NOT WANT TO OBSTRUCT his nakedness. I KNOW if I WALK directly toward him, I WILL block him, so I LOOK to the director for cues. He WINKS and says, "Just be natural."

I WALK slowly toward the handsome man, savoring the sight of his nakedness and my own growing sensuality. I FINGER my gossamer dress, delighting in the fact that I am clothed and he is not. I TANTALIZE myself by imagining his response if I were to JOIN him in the nude.

When I am about three feet from him, I STOP. He LOOKS toward me and smiles. I KNOW the soul that awaits behind his smile. He RESPONDS to the soul that makes its home in my body. I CATCH a fleeting breath, WANTING this moment to last forever.

Initial Reflections:

I am ready to receive my inner partner. I know that my sexuality is filled with power. Until now, passion has been my shadow, for expressing it has led to dire consequences. I desire to be loved and loving in the ways of this dream.

Polarities include male–female, clothed–naked, and aroused–restrained.

In a follow-up conversation with my dream guide, she commented that the image I described sounded like the lover card in the Tarot deck. "So, Rosalie, who is the director?"

Without hesitating, I replied, "God." Embarrassed, I searched for a more mundane association, but none came to mind.

"So God is directing you to be natural?" Ellise asked.

"So it seems," I said, with more reserve than I felt.

"And the naked man's name?"

"Generosity," I replied, grateful that this man was so different from the young boy.

"And what is your name in the dream?"

"Truth," I said, with genuine delight.

Had I thought before responding, I would have reported that the man's name was Truth and the woman's Generosity. After all, I'd always regarded truth as a masculine characteristic and generosity, or nurturance, as a feminine one. Perhaps I am becoming androgynous!

This inner integration feels promising. Time will tell if this dream also predicts a future encounter.

(1996) Ascending and Landing

I AM CLIMBING a high, rugged mountain. As I near the peak, I feel exhausted and UNABLE TO GO FARTHER. My only option is to LET GO and crash to earth. As I RELEASE my grip, PREPARING TO BE PULVERIZED, I am terrified. To my amazement, however, I LAND feet first on the soft earth and AWAKE with the words "Another perfect landing" on my lips.

Initial Reflections:

Whew! I've had close calls before, but this one was too close. My terror felt real. What am I afraid of? I know I am being asked to trust more, but trust what? Hanging on to common sense no longer serves me. Besides, something else moves within me, and although my mind is adamant in convincing me of impending danger, my unconscious has a different message.

Polarities include ascent–descent, fear–trust, and surrender–terror. In honor of this dream I will practice surrendering to the unknown and trusting my ability to survive.

(1997) On the Edge Again

(THIS DREAM SLIPPED INTO MY CONSCIOUS MIND IN BITS AND PIECES. I WILL
RECORD IT IN THE SEQUENCE IN WHICH IT EMERGED — THE LAST PIECE FIRST, AND
THEN THE BEGINNING, COMING AS A FLASHBACK.)

I am almost at the top of a gigantic mountain. Looking far below,
I CAN BARELY MAKE OUT a friend SWIMMING in a large pool. She BECKONS me
to join her. I refuse and CONTINUE TO CLIMB.

When my destination is almost within reach, I HEAR voices from
the top of the mountain. "HELP!" I SCREAM. Then I REALIZE I WILL HAVE TO
LET GO of the precipice with one arm so I can BE ASSISTED to the top.
I AM DETERMINED to join these people.

They look down at me from about two feet overhead. They YELL
words I DO NOT UNDERSTAND. Apparently, nobody here COMMUNICATES in
English, and I speak no other language.

I am INVITED to address a gathering of people. There a woman
asks if I WILL speak about her child's soul purpose. I PAUSE and ATTUNE
to my guides. They INSTRUCT me to talk to the group about questing.
I SPEAK from my heart and AM FILLED with passion and joy.

Initial Reflections:

This dream reminds me of Psyche's last labor, which demanded that
she prioritize her own work over the caretaking of others. I do soul
readings easily, and I am in demand. Yet superseding this calling is
another one — the quest itself. In the dream I am determined. For
this Pisces woman to say no to water is monumental.

The folks on top do not speak my language, nor do I understand
theirs. More and more, I am speaking the language of energy, which
feels like the dialect of the divine. Often, I have no words to express the
fullness of my experience. To be assisted in the quest, I must let go.

Polarities include determination–receptivity, prioritizing–
accommodating, and giving–receiving.

Although this dream has no outcome, I am hopeful. I am so near
the top — in my life, as well. I am breaking through limitations at last!

Invitation to Write

After bundling your dream crop, along with your initial reflections on each episode, you can harness deeper meanings by working sequentially with the words you have underlined. Navigating your way through the underworld is a three-step process. To begin, chart the underlined phrases or sentences beneath the date and title of each dream. Here is Rosalie's chart:

(1985) ESSENCE

~ *White rose essence*

~ *I can buy more essence*

~ *I giggle*

~ *For the moment, it is enough for me to know*

(1991) THE SURPRISE OFFERING

~ *I feel vulnerable and excited*

~ *I no longer have passion for the course I agreed to teach*

~ *I plan to teach something new*

~ *Everyone elects to stay in a course that is still under development*

(1992) THE FUTURE

~ *In a different state*

~ *A calendar marked March 7, 2007*

~ *En route to Me.*

~ *I like the spirit of this out-of-body adventure*

(1994) THE KISS

~ *I enjoy his kiss, which feels more playful than sexual*

~ *I do not understand why they are so concerned, but I sense it is connected with the kiss*

~ *To me, the kiss is simply a spontaneous gesture*

~ *Available for unexpected times of magic and awakening*

(1995) DESPERATE SEARCH

∾I am nervous, because I am in charge of his safety and he is a daredevil

∾We dive deep down to reach him, but he seems to have disappeared

(1995) THE DREAM CALL

∾I am fascinated by the play of light

∾"I don't need your invitation; I'll come whenever I like."

∾I am astounded that I have been out of control

∾I struggle to be my grown-up self

∾"I also own this home, and I am in charge."

∾"Lady, you can invite me if you want, but I'll come back whenever I feel like it."

(1995) INTEGRATION

∾I do not want to obstruct his nakedness

∾Savoring the sight of his nakedness and my growing sensuality

∾I know the soul that awaits behind his smile

(1996) ASCENDING AND LANDING

∾I am climbing

∾I release my grip, preparing to be pulverized

∾I land feet first on the soft earth

(1997) ON THE EDGE AGAIN

∾I will have to let go of the precipice with one arm so I can be assisted to the top

∾Nobody here communicates in English, and I speak no other language

Second, when your chart is complete, write as many paragraphs as you wish, using one phrase or sentence from each dream. Here is Rosalie's dream harvest:

For the moment, it is enough for me to know I plan to teach something new. I feel vulnerable when I admit that I wish to teach people about essence.

"There's plenty of time," my dreams counsel. "Take a look — on the wall is a calendar marked March 7, 2007."

Being available for unexpected times of magic and awakening means I must speak from my own experience. Often, I remind myself that I am a daredevil who enjoys watching the play of light. I am also savoring my sensuality. Others try to rescue me from the kiss of essence, but I am beyond their reach.

Ascending and landing are practical skills I am learning. I am amazed each time I land feet first on the soft earth. I am determined to learn whatever I need to know — even if I will have to let go of the precipice with one arm so I can be assisted to the top.

Finally, to draw sustaining nourishment from your dreams, complete the reflective writing exercise described on pages 41–42. Here are Rosalie's responses:

- **I LEARNED** that my unconscious is telling me what to attend to and that it is persistent. On some nights two or more dreams will all illustrate the same theme!

- **I RELEARNED** that dreams are my teachers. They remind me, confront me with, comfort me, and prepare me for the future. I am a student of dreams.

- **I DISCOVERED** how ready I am to listen, cooperate, and embrace the unknown. Conventional thinking, teaching, and behaving no longer interest me. I am a quester.

- **I REGRET** nothing!

- **I APPRECIATE** the patience I exhibit in my dreams. I also appreciate my willingness to risk taking action on messages revealed in my dreams.

- **RIGHT NOW I FEEL** filled with energy and possibilities.

- **AND I WILL** continue to record my dreams, striving always to remain receptive to spirit by night and by day.

Next time you enter the fields to gather dreams, imagine that you hold in your writing hand a magic dream net similar to a butterfly net. Capture dreams that choose you. Be receptive to those that intrigue you. Bundle up and write about those that seem to illuminate the path you are on.

Use the following quotations as inspiration while writing about your dreams:

"The best way to make your dreams come true is to wake up."   — Kabir

"When we take time to dream, we discover the many windows to our soul."
— Isabela Barani

"When an inner situation is not made conscious, it happens outside as fate."
— Carl Jung

"We are all vulnerable to the unexplored."   —The Talmud

Creativity

After more than twenty years of researching, teaching, and writing about creativity, I discovered that learning to be more creative isn't a weekend workshop job; it's an ongoing process that eventually touches every aspect of our existence. In the beginning I focused on methods and techniques. Random word input, metaphorical connection-making, force-fit grids, and other tricks of the trade easily sparked new ideas; communication skills helped people think more effectively *together*. From there I moved on to study the psychological aspects of creative behavior. It was all heady stuff, and I loved it. As I broke old habits and took more risks, the lights came up in my world. Everything seemed brighter, more interesting, and connected in marvelous new ways.

Now I can't imagine teaching or writing anything that isn't enriched by freshness, spontaneity, and other creative principles. While tracking how my thinking about creativity changed over the years, I discovered a path that led from the head to the heart.

FEBRUARY 10, 1985

"A problem is simply the difference between what you have and what you want." I found these words inscribed on a napkin tucked between the pages of a journal I kept as a graduate student years ago. I have no idea where they came from, and no memory of having written them. Nevertheless, I've been saying them all this time.

In countless creativity workshops, I've noticed that people typically have less trouble describing the "what you have" than they do imagining the "what you want." The first part can be researched, and often measured. The challenge lies in moving the second part from Band-Aid–level creativity ("Make it stop hurting..." "Put it back the way it was..." "Just fix it!") to breakthrough creativity ("Let's seize this opportunity to move way ahead of where we are!"). Essentially, my task has been to help people figure out what they want to create in place of what they have.

JULY 29, 1985

At long last, it feels easy to respond from a positive, forward-looking stance. It's become natural to say things like, "How can we make this work?" rather than, "That won't work because..." It's now second nature to turn complaints into problems to be solved and to turn negative statements into opportunities to be seized.

SEPTEMBER 7, 1989

We can't LEARN creativity like we learn algebra. It's not a neat and tidy finite body of knowledge. We can EXPLORE creativity, however, and as we do, the inevitable learning will be about ourselves. That's because in the process we explore what we want, what we value, and what our purpose may be. We then discover how we block ourselves and how we set ourselves free and how important it is to love and care for ourselves. It works best if we explore with a sense of curiosity, playfulness, and self-acceptance. Banish blame, guilt, and judgment —they get you stuck every time.

I must remember that to grow, the teacher has to remain a student. Indeed, I seem to teach what I most need to learn.

FEBRUARY 20, 1990

What happens when I make a metaphorical connection? I gain a creative perspective by looking at things differently. Whether it happens in poetry, science, or life itself, the process is the same: a surge of energy loosens rigid assumptions, opening up new possibilities and deepening my understanding.

One of my favorite games is to randomly pick an object and begin looking for a similarity between it and me. A slightly repulsive object is the greatest challenge of all. At first, I usually cannot find a connection; my mind is still stuck in its carefully constructed categories of things "like me" and "not like me." Then as I decompartmentalize my thinking, I am able to see in the object qualities that *do* describe me.

For example, as I sit here in a dingy airport terminal, a discarded rubber glove blows about outside, near the glass door leading to the tarmac. However much the wind tosses and tumbles it, the glove never loses its shape. When the wind dies down, it floats gracefully back to the concrete walkway, with all five finger sections intact. This reminds me of my own resilience. From time to time, winds buffet my being, yet my sense of myself returns unscathed.

I've taught metaphoric thinking to hundreds of scientists and businesspeople. For some it's hard going at first; their minds have things so neatly categorized that they rebel at the thought of dissolving the pigeonholes. Finally discovering a connection, they smile and their eyes light up. If metaphors bring happiness and eradicate alienation, could reawakening the metaphoric mind draw people together in peace?

MARCH 4, 1992

"It's like what Jung meant by the 'collective unconscious.' Only in my mind it not only takes in the past and all of human knowledge, I think it takes in the future. I think it takes in other worlds. I think it takes in the language of trees and animals. What's important about that is the imagination is a real place. We simply have to learn how to enter into it." — Deena Metzger

Deena's words remind me of the realm of imagination I too often lose touch with, and of why writing beyond reason is so very reasonable. How sensible it is to fill my journal pages with nonsense, for how else will I discover what I didn't know I knew?

This afternoon a workshop participant asked me to describe the three most important things I'd discovered about creativity. I said, "Tame your judgmental mind by looking for possibilities. Reawaken your curiosity and imagination, both of which will help you outrun your judgmental self. And always look for connections between seemingly unrelated things, since nothing is unrelated when you're looking for new ideas."

As for me, I have to work at being proactive instead of reactive. Maybe that's the same as taming judgment and looking for unexpected associations. When I remember to shift from talking, thinking, or writing about what I DON'T WANT to contemplating what I DO WANT, my energy shifts. I begin to look forward, instead of backward. I feel clear and alive — signs of a creative principle at work.

MAY 6, 1992

Today I wrote a description of the session Rosalie and I will co-facilitate on exploring friendship as a support for creative growth. While outlining my understanding of the relationship between friendship and creativity, I realized that Rosalie and I have stayed connected over thousands of miles for fifteen years by holding each other's stories. Creating friendships should be considered an art form and accorded as much praise as creating novels, paintings, and poems.

FEBRUARY 25, 1993

I often write about the joys of discovering creativity. I need to honor the darker aspects, too — the fact that the creative process can also take us into the proverbial pits. There come times when we must fight for our creative life. There come times when we face disappointment, frustration, and failure.

I do best when I release my anxiety about outcomes and focus on trusting the process while appreciating its ups and downs, its twists and turns. Trusting the creative process has led me to trusting the mystery of life.

MARCH 18, 1993

Yesterday I listened to a taped interview with psychiatrist Thomas Moore. His thoughts about the shadow side of creativity reminded me of the vague, "stuck again" feelings I've whined about in countless journals. Had I no conscious longing to be brilliantly expressive or to produce a worthy manuscript, I think there'd be few frustra-tions in my life. Well, not quite — I could always obsess about my organizationally challenged mind and my cluttered office and the boxes of old photographs I never get around to sorting through!

Purposefully pursuing creativity raises twin expectations. For one, sensing new possibilities brings zest to my life. The other side I encounter when I disappoint myself by not coming up with many innovative ideas. Moore reminds me that during such interludes the creative spark is NOT gone forever. Instead, this fallow time pre-pares the fields while seeds lie dormant. It's all part of the process.

APRIL 16, 1993

I've come to understand that creative process is not about creating something separate from myself; it's about creating WHO I AM. I create myself through my creations.

NOVEMBER 2, 1993

Creativity is our natural state. Refuse it and the life goes out of us.

Could suppressed creativity be feeding the anger that erupts into violence in our cities' streets? Where does it come from, all this violence? Perhaps it flows out of homes where children aren't allowed to daydream. Or maybe our own disappointments and frus-trations, hopelessness and despair have infected our young. Some days the only power many of them see is violence, hatred, and destruction.

Imagine a world in which every child could say: "I matter. I belong here. My life has purpose. I can create, and together with others, I can make a difference. I have songs to sing, a poem to write, a picture to paint of a brighter tomorrow, a family and friends to help, and a planet to live on in harmony." How different would things be then?

NOVEMBER 12, 1993

"No one does anything of great significance because they have to," a French hang-glider pilot and extreme skier said on a *National Geographic* special I watched last night on TV. I think he's right.

Although we may say we HAD to write this story, paint this picture, or create this organization, what we really mean is our passion compelled us to create something we longed to bring into being. Manifesting something new is never a "should" or a "must" taken on as a mantle of duty; it's a joy emanating from the natural flow of intention.

JUNE 22, 1994

Things I've learned about creativity:

 ~ Resistance has meaning, and discovering it leads to choice. Resistance is the symptom; meaning is the cause. Honor the resistance and search for the cause. On the other side of resistance lie the words that most need to be said.

 ~ I am my own worst critic, even when I don't speak in clichés!

 ~ Inner stillness often evokes revelation.

 ~ I will never be as good as I want to be or as bad as I fear I'll be.

 ~ Always be open to unexpected outcomes.

Here's what I understand right now: Behind fear is powerlessness. When I fight down my fear, I'm fighting off feelings of powerlessness. Powerlessness blocks creativity.

Thus, tapping into my power will free creativity. By power, I do not mean the impulse to control and command, but rather the strength that comes from maintaining trust in my deep knowing and in the higher powers I'm connected to. I have the power to choose curiosity over judgment, trust over fear, compassion over resentment — and when I make those shifts, I connect to the life force and reclaim my vitality.

Each time I quiet myself and expand my receptivity, I make a space for information, insights, and new ideas to flow in. Much more comes through this approach than through focused, determined, goal-directed thinking. Intuition doesn't work that way.

JUNE 23, 1994

Focus on what's working and it will grow. Worry about what's not working and it, too, will grow. Free your imagination to explore what you want in place of what you've got and you can usually get unstuck.

Other ways to get unstuck:

∿ Act as if you already have what you want.

∿ Just show up and do what's next.

∿ Do nothing out of fear — act with intention.

∿ Ask, "What if...?"

∿ Remember that being stuck comes with the territory! It is part of the creative process.

NOVEMBER 20, 1994

A man calls looking for a tools-and-techniques workshop. The conversation reveals that he's looking for a quick fix — ten easy steps to creativity and innovation. I talk to him about context, about how learning is enhanced when creative-thinking tools are taught within a context that helps people understand WHY they work. Then they can use those tools more effectively. "How long does that take?" Whatever I say will be too long for him. The real answer? It takes a lifetime, AND we never get it completely.

APRIL 10, 1995 (AS MY NEW GRANDDAUGHTER, ANNA, SLEEPS AT MY FEET)

Creativity is about much more than new art, music, literature, or science. What we are ultimately creating is our own lives — for better or worse, artfully or crudely, consciously or unconsciously. By understanding how the most routine task fits into the life we're shaping, we can behold it as a creative act. Label it boring and that's what it will be; connect it to purpose and energy rises to ennoble it.

Watching little Anna sleep feels creative. Tiny glints of red in her dark brown hair remind me of my auburn-haired Grandmother Robinson. Every now and then Anna sucks on the big rubber pacifier she became addicted to in the intensive care neonatal unit where she spent her first few weeks on earth. Then she settles back into sleep. Remembering how close we came to losing her, I breathe in my gratitude that she gets to stay with us and breathe out my thanks. I wonder if she's dreaming.

Soon her big brother, Adam, will come home, and we'll play with his blocks and trains. How I wish we adults were more childlike while creating our lives! Children construct all sorts of things with blocks and then knock them down to see what else they can do with them. We, on the other hand, build a new form and then strive to keep it just as it is. WE FORGET WE'RE ONLY PLAYING. We think that what we've arranged so conceptually is what is instead of being merely one possibility among many. Today, I'll knock down some blocks just for fun.

MAY 10, 1996

Found in the margin of an entry dated March 3, 1993: "Every act of creation is an act of faith."

I don't know who said that, but since there are quotes around it, I know it wasn't me. Seeing it there, I add, "Yes!" Showing up every morning to write is an act of faith. No matter how discouraged or confused I am, the fact that I show up tells me that my faith is strong, even if I feel wobbly.

I used to believe creativity was about THINGS — books, paintings, discoveries, inventions. Now I know creativity is about the heart. I used to think of creativity as a gift some of us have and some of us don't. Now I believe creativity is our life force, our connection to spirit.

Found in the back of the same journal: "I'm tired of the aggressive, mechanistic masculine metaphors that many business groups use habitually, and no doubt unconsciously. I believe that the metaphors we employ to think about issues profoundly affect our perceptions. One group that consistently uses hostile metaphors to describe its clients is, ironically enough, working on ways to improve client relationships!"

Why not use natural, organic metaphors? Or the "feminine" metaphors spawned by chaos theory? Or curds and whey, smooth noodle maps, fudge flakes, cups, dust, and webs? What might these reveal? What if we were to challenge the metaphors we use for hidden prejudices and unconscious assumptions? What if we were to purposefully use powerful metaphors to bring our vision alive and remind us of our purpose, focus our energy, and move us forward?

APRIL 15, 1996

We forget we've created this world and can therefore re-create it differently. Instead, we consider ourselves uncreative and behave accordingly. How do we create our world? With our thoughts! We live in the movies of our minds, unaware that we're actors in a cosmic play we've cocreated. Of course, we can't always control what happens, but we CAN control our response to it. Responding is different from reacting.

SEPTEMBER 4, 1996

The soul does two things: it loves and it creates. Those are its two primary acts, according to Sue Monk Kidd, author of *Dance of the Dissident Daughter.*

Then there's Jack Hawley, author of *Reawakening the Spirit in Business,* who says, "Dive deeply enough into any subject and the questions that shimmer before you are spiritual."

A long time ago Ted, Rosalie, and I came to the conclusion that if you start exploring CREATIVITY beyond its surface tricks, it will inevitably lead you to both INTUITION and SPIRITUALITY. Ted called these terms the "three sisters."

MARCH 28, 1997

Apparently, our thoughts about the "three sisters" weren't all that original! In an *Intuition* magazine interview with cultural anthropologist Angeles Arrien, she mentions finding this footnote in the work of Theodore Riser, who conducted cross-cultural studies in the 1930s: "There are three words that come up in all languages and they seem to be synonymous: INTUITION, SPIRITUALITY, and CREATIVITY." More and more I am discovering that all our "new" thinking is foreshadowed, if not directly expressed, in words of the ancients.

Angeles, journeying down the same path we've traveled, goes on to say: "I thought about this for a long time. A person who chooses a spiritual path can't avoid intuition and becoming more creative." Well, I DIDN'T choose the spiritual path first; I began with creativity. That led me to intuition, and then spirituality. I imagine the three sisters in a circle. If you begin dancing with whichever one initially attracts you, she will twirl you around to the other two.

MARCH 21, 1997

How can we move beyond blame and judgment? How can we remind ourselves that most flawed ideas aren't wrong, just incomplete? How might we move beyond right-wrong or good-bad and still be ethical? By telling the truth as we experience it and by being kind.

"Kill an absurd idea and you've also killed the brilliant one it might have led you to." I said these words in today's workshop and then ran to write them down before they evaporated!

JUNE 25, 1998 (AFTER WALKING A LABYRINTH)

While walking the ancient path, I realize how far from the center I am just before a wide arc throws me into it. Somewhere en route I get scared — afraid I've taken a wrong turn and will be thrown out before reaching the center. Then just when I think I've completed the return, I'm blocked from the straight path out and must make another loop. Along the way, my awareness invariably strays back to the office and I'm working on my "to do" list instead of being present. Always, there's an unexpected AHA! This time I heard: "Why are you so surprised by the confusion and uncertainty of the stuck times in your writing — and your life for that matter? They're both creative processes, so how could it be otherwise?"

Reflective Writing:

~ I LEARNED that all my journals hold thoughts about creativity.

~ I RELEARNED that creativity works best in the service of purpose. Put the WHY before the WHAT and HOW.

~ I DISCOVERED numerous entries pointing to failure of imagination as a root cause of unhappiness and despair.

~ I REDISCOVERED the exhilarating sense of rebirth I felt when I first explored my own creativity.

~ I REGRET that I was nearly forty when I finally realized it was possible to reclaim my creativity and purposefully develop it.

~ I APPRECIATE that I've learned to trust the creative process and not worry when life gets confusing or when I feel stuck.

~ RIGHT NOW I FEEL that parts of the creative process call for feminine energy and other parts draw forth masculine energy.

~**AND I WILL** help my grandchildren hold on to each facet of their creative spirits, all the while nurturing my own.

Invitation to Write

What role does creativity play in your life? How important is it to you? When have you been most creative? What blocks your creativity and gets you stuck? What purpose does your creativity serve? What would you most like to create for yourself at this point in life? What can you do to keep your creativity alive and well? How might you encourage others to develop their creativity?

Here are some insights to spark new thoughts:

"*I love myself more than I love cooperating with my own oppression. Abuse our children and social services will show up. Abuse our pets and the Humane Society will. Why is there no 'creativity patrol' or 'soul police' to protect us?*"
— Clarissa Pinkola Éstes

"*When we leave art only to 'artists,' we lose touch with our own artfulness, our creativity and inventiveness, and block a portal through which great vigor and intelligence can make their way to us.*" — Gregg Levoy

"*When you can't go forward and you can't go backward and you can't stay where you are without killing what's deep and vital — you are on the edge of creation.*" — Sue Monk Kidd

"*I can always be distracted by love, but eventually I get horny for my creativity.*"
— Guilda Radner

10

Love

FROM ROSALIE'S JOURNALS

Rereading my journals, I've discovered that love has stalked me for decades! Sometimes I recorded finding my connection to love through relationships; other times I wrote about the core of love. Still other times I struggled with the lifelong process of loving myself. The years 1977 to 1979, after the sudden death of my son Mike, were traumatic for me. I questioned everything I had believed and everything I had been taught. Slowly, a new way of being grew in my journal entries.

AUGUST 1978

Yesterday someone asked me what my heart's desire was. I replied, without thinking, "To be loved and loving."

APRIL 1979

Love is forgiving; forgiveness precedes wholeness.

I have not forgiven myself or God for Mike's sudden death. Wholeness is nowhere in sight. So what is this stuff about love and forgiveness? Who is responsible for this cryptic sentence? All I know is that the hole in the middle of my heart will always be part of my wholeness.

MAY 1980

The lessons are always about love. What matters is only what you give with love.

Where do these platitudes come from? All my life I have been dutiful, responsible, somewhat obedient to several cultural imperatives. What do I know about love? Yet the words linger in my mind, visit me throughout the day, invade my consciousness at night. What matters most is that I heal. It feels as if somebody is handing me a map. But who?

SEPTEMBER 1981

I lack a model for intimacy. Before I can be intimate with someone else, I need to be honest with myself. I do not want to share myself half digested. Where did I adopt the notion about not trusting a lover to accept me unless I have myself all together? When I am honest with myself, I admit that the only love I am lonely for is love of self.

NOVEMBER 1981

True celebration springs from love.

Have I been present to celebrate love? Yes, with my sister friends I outrageously embrace love and joy. With a man, I hesitate.

JULY 1983

Trust love to be as limitless as consciousness.

I want to trust love. I have experienced the boundlessness of consciousness. But (always the *BUT*) all my life, older people have told me that love heals. Do I dare to believe that?

NOVEMBER 1985

Although I've never imagined myself a poet, I awoke early this morning in the midst of a poem:

> *Love restores.*
> *Love initiates flow.*
> *Love ignites.*
> *Love loves.*
> *Love is the channel.*
> *You are the form.*

Less and less am I able to tell the difference between my thoughts and ideas channeled from my guides.

DECEMBER 1985

My guides have apparently agreed to instruct me in the ways of love during the night. Instead of a one-liner, paragraphs appear. I must be quite a project!

Love is the transformer and the transforming. Be willing to lead with love, for it is the energy of love that engages the universal mind. When you lift your energies from your human heart to your high heart — the center midway between your human heart and throat — you attract essence. Your loving attitude serves as an antenna. Then your assignment is to translate the energetic impressions you receive into words and, later, concepts. Always, the first step is to extend love from your high heart.

This resonance automatically aligns you with "spaciousness." As you merge with spaciousness, you attract the attention of your guides as well as the wisdom of your soul. Do this daily. It requires discipline, devotion, and a certain amount of duty.

This is making sense. I believe I have been catching information from my guides and teachers for a while. However, I did not know how to connect with them consciously; nobody handed me a rule book. Even though I have only half understood their guidance, I have written every piece of information in my journals. Without love, I would not be who I am.

MAY 1991

Many insights sparked me during my three-day retreat at a local convent. I realized that as I live with love, I evoke spirit. All the lessons are about love.

When I dare to lead with love, I express spirit. Attuning to the presence of love in everything I do, I become a student of spirit.

SEPTEMBER 1991

As I sink deeper into the peace and power of high heart, I hear the whisperings of my inner voice:

Love is as vast as beauty is wide. Love does not attach itself to particular people or places. Instead it permeates ever outward, fostered as it is by loving.

You travel to New Mexico to expand. Yet in doing so, you do not leave home behind, because home is the sacredness that resides in your heart.

This is true. During my move from Maine, where I had lived for forty-seven years, to El Salto Mountain in northern New Mexico, love grounded me.

SEPTEMBER 1991

I have worked since I was eleven years old. Dare I love myself enough to give myself this year off as a gift? I remember "catching" the notion that love is forgiving, and I trust that applies to me loving myself.

OCTOBER 1991

For the past month I have been repeating the affirmation "Love guides my life." Today I realized the affirmation has become as natural as breathing. People respond to the love I extend. I smile at strangers and feel love returned. This morning I surprised the UPS man with a hug. Daily, I experience love, express it, and remain present as it returns to me.

My teaching, too, is filled with love, ease, and humor. Explanations come spontaneously, without thinking. I challenge, provoke, share, and simply entertain with stories. Dare I believe that I can merely be present and loving?

"What about lesson plans?" my trickster cajoles.

Lesson plans leave no room for love and the unexpected.

JANUARY 1992

How do I begin to explain that the more you love, the more you activate the divinity in matter? From deep in my soul I know that life serves love and love serves life and both are in service to evolution.

JANUARY 1992

Before flying to Florida for a conference, I went for a Tarot reading, where I was told I would return from Florida in a committed relationship.

"Committed to what?" I asked.

"A man," she replied.

Could this relate to a daring remark I made last week, wondering what it would feel like to be pursued by a man? Perhaps the universe heard my words. Well, I'm NOT READY. I take it all back.

FEBRUARY 1992

The first night of the International Light Link Conference I had a dream that I was traveling around the world teaching and networking with other healers. Before long, we had formed a multicultural healing center where healers and teachers were collaborating, synthesizing the best of our work. I awoke feeling excited, for this has been a longtime soul desire of mine.

In the breakfast line the following morning, I turned around and Michael, a man I had met in my dream, smiled at me. It was then that I remembered I had not been traveling alone. In my natural, outgoing way, I shared the dream with him. He listened respectfully and then excused himself. Later, he said he thought I was just giving him a line.

All week Michael and I danced in the mornings to Panurhythmia, and took walks and played together. Before I left, he asked me to travel and teach with him. I was scared of making another mistake by trusting a man. Although he wanted to leave for Europe immediately, I put him off until September.

On my drive back from the conference, I dared the radio to spell out the meaning of my relationship with Michael; the next song, I challenged, would tell me what was going on. Johnny Mathis crooned, "When I fall in love, it will be forever." I switched the dial until all I could pick up was static. Then pulling over to the side of the highway, I reminded myself to breathe. Any other song would have been welcomed, but not my favorite tune as a vulnerable teenager, before I knew what love was. Dare I trust again?

Michael moved from Florida to Taos three weeks after we met. Hence, true to the Tarot reading, I returned to Taos in a committed relationship — but one filled with questions.

APRIL 1992

Can love, power, peace, and purpose be sustained in a relationship? I have experienced all these phenomena while in partnership, but only fleetingly. My focus has been less on what relationship offers my partner than on what it offers the world. Even so, I have felt alone in my desire to bring something to the world from partnership.

Can the world benefit from an intimate relationship? This is still a question I entertain. I suppose the only way to find an answer is to plunge in fully...again.

MAY 1992

Quietness visited me today. Silence feels as natural to me as the rhythm of labor pains announcing the birth of a baby. As my body reorients to silence, my heart whispers, my limbs relax, and I sink my ass into the cradle of the earth. From this centered place, I know without doubt that all interactions are either extensions of love or projections of fear. It is truly that simple.

JUNE 1992

I am realizing the difference between an attitude and a judgment. I display my attitude when I disagree with someone and continue to be loving toward them; I slide into judgment when I disagree and withhold love. For example, Kelli-Lynne and I frequently disagree, but if I were to judge her, I'd no longer be available to love her. I must remember this distinction, because I come from a family in which people guard their grudges and horde their love like precious gems.

JUNE 1992

This morning Audrey, my spiritual mother, reminded me that fear is the opposite of faith. I know from personal experience that faith, like love, springs from the heart. Perhaps we can find ways to talk about a change of heart like we do a change of mind.

JUNE 1993

I need to write about what I am FEELING as well as what I am FEARING in relationship. I withstand limited amounts of intimacy, and then I create a confrontation...The word WITHSTAND surprises me. How long have I associated intimacy with something to be tolerated? The truth is I get scared. Then I retreat or write or walk — anything to reclaim my space. Today I even cleaned up the house!

I fear that relationship does not allow me enough room to express my creativity. I also carry the sabotaging belief that I cannot trust a man to make room for my essence. Was I denied self-expression in my family? An enormous sigh erupts from the bottom of my belly in response to the question. While growing up, if I dared to say, "I want..." I was summarily dismissed or humiliated. To avoid ridicule, I began providing for myself.

Whenever I get scared, my family history kicks in and I respond with stubbornness, moving away from my heart. Then I further defend myself by uttering mean words and backing them up with retaliatory actions. I also wipe out all memories of how safe I feel in Michael's arms.

Protecting myself from loving and being loved makes no sense. Why am I acting this way? The love I knew as a child was conditional, and was withdrawn on a whim, especially when I did not conform to parental wishes. My conclusion: allowing myself to be loved is not worth the effort it takes. Trailing immediately behind this decision comes another learned limitation: my love doesn't count, and it is just a matter of time before someone else I love leaves.

At this moment I feel like running away, even closing this journal — definite signs of resistance. Could I be avoiding intimacy at all costs? I do know I am committed to healing within relationship, and that means releasing these dysfunctional patterns.

Okay, I'm clearer now, more grown up too. The time has come to make amends and be gentle with myself...

I apologized to Michael for being combative and protective of myself. He hugged me, accepted my apology, and reiterated that he did not enjoy battling with me. Later, I stopped at a flower shop and bought a long-stemmed red rose for him — signifying my sincere desire to be present in relationship.

JULY 1993

Why does it feel as though I am betraying my women friends by being in a relationship with a man? My guilt feels archetypal. Worse yet, I am having to eat my words about the impossibility of a conscious relationship existing between a man and a woman.

Such deep scars I carry! I wonder if I am addicted to pain while in relationship?

AUGUST 1993

Today I am aware of being more disciplined about attitudes. It reminds me of weeding a garden; first, I must be able to tell the difference between the weeds (attitudes) and the flowers (love). I surprised myself by writing the following:

 ∾ Adopt a loving attitude upon waking.

 ∾ Entertain loving thoughts throughout the day.

 ∾ Embrace others with love.

 ∾ Before drifting off to sleep, review the love surrounding you
   throughout the day.

(Note: Michael and I stayed together for nearly two years, throughout which time he remained ever present, insisting that I feel my feelings. Too much togetherness, however, created a dilemma for me: I needed more space. We soon became critical of each other, and I knew I was no longer expressing the essence of love. With his belongings in my by now swelling storage unit, I left, committing myself to a "relationship fast" and a full year of celibacy.)

JANUARY 1994

Author Maggie Scarff believes that in partnership each person must be comfortable expressing their need for both intimacy and autonomy. Looking back, I can see I have majored in autonomy. One day, when Michael frustratingly asked me what I wanted from a relationship, I replied without thinking, "Space and flowers." He sighed, and when I asked him the same question he answered, "Intimacy."

FEBRUARY 1994

Love and abundance are two aspects of the same impulse. I yearn to love with an open heart and open hands, which means wishing always for the highest good of my beloved and myself. Although this is my desire, I am not yet able to accomplish it in partnership. At this point in my life, I choose to be monogamous with myself!

MARCH 1994

Last night I spent delicious hours with two women friends, Chris and Sherry. We have a great deal in common: we are single by choice, we delight in living near mountains, we are transplants to New

Mexico, and we are developing a sense of entitlement as well as empowerment.

Our conversation centered on relationships. Each of us in turn addressed the question "What's in it for me when a man invites me to join him for supper, a movie, sex, or life?" We found that basing our decisions on the question "Is it sweet enough?" gives rise to new behavior.

Each of us had something profound to share. Someone had tutored Chris in saying, simply, "It doesn't work for me" — a statement no one can argue with. Sherry talked about how casually men say "I love you" and expect a woman to respond with open legs. I explained that I felt as if I had released centuries of cultural conditioning by refusing to feel special each time a man makes a speck of space for me in his life.

No longer do I need a man to provide for me. Actually, no man ever did; in all my relationships I have provided for myself and my partner. Ultimately, coupling seems more confining than confirming, more restrictive than expansive. I know how to manifest and do not need a man to do that for me. I know how to appreciate myself. I even know how to pleasure myself sexually! Reveling in life WITHOUT a man is revolutionary in my family of origin.

MARCH 1994
The men I've been in partnership with have wanted my radiance for themselves, and yet my purpose has been to encourage them to be in THEIR essence. To tell the truth, I am more comfortable with universal love than with its personal variations. For me, a partner must be at ease in his own light.

APRIL 1994
The wisdom in the aphorism "Wherever I go, I meet myself" struck deep chords in me while I met with a forty-year-old doctor whose soul purpose is to learn about personal love and come to peace with the human experience. He was a mirror for me, especially when he said, "I am tired of women hugging me with their arms when I want to be hugged by their souls."

He asked me to tell him what women wanted. Before I had framed my thoughts, however, he said, "I want a woman who lives in her power and her light and knows that her source of power comes not from me, but from light itself." I smiled, grateful that someone had put into words what I, too, require in a relationship.

APRIL 1994
Commotion surrounded me today. The landlord made outrageous demands of me; the car wouldn't start; Kelli-Lynne was grouchy because her boyfriend didn't call; and I was impatient to write in my journal. Love felt like an endangered species.

MAY 1994
> *Love.*
> *Love love.*
> *Love your bones.*
> *Love the stories of being human.*
> *Love the silences.*
> *Love the life you have created.*
> *Love its perplexity as well as its simplicity.*
> *Love the loving*
> *Together with all that exists in the crucible of love*
> *Until love becomes all.*

I feel like adding, "Until love becomes a habit." How different it is to act out of love — such as when I call my grandmother each week, or take Kelli-Lynne into town for extra school supplies, or make chicken soup for a sick friend — than out of duty!

JUNE 1994
Today, people described me as "glowing" and assumed I was in love. I know that whenever I make myself irresistible to spirit, I radiate love. Blowing bubbles, hiking, snorkeling, making love, and arranging flowers are some of my favorite ways to engage the attention of my guides and teachers.

As a teenager, whenever I dared to broadcast love, I attracted plenty of sexual attention. Because I hadn't a clue about how to handle responses from men of all ages, I eventually shut down my passion for life. At fifty, I am no longer willing to compromise this desire to be in relationship with life as a lover.

SEPTEMBER 1995

I feel different now that I now longer define myself as part of a couple. I feel more peaceful, spontaneous, free, focused, appreciative of my life. I feel more competent, more generous to myself and my friends, more devoted to spiritual realities, more in touch with my body.

I wonder if I will ever choose to be in a committed relationship again. Each time I have entered into one, I have trusted that both my partner and I would continue to respect the demands and delights of our souls' journeys. And each time, my heart has been shattered.

As I reflect on the men I have loved, I see a pattern: they have remained somewhat aloof. Initially, I was attracted to each one because of his aura of being in control. I suspect I have misinterpreted detachment for inner peace. Michael, however, was different; he was always present, which scared me. I'd had no experience matching a man who was my equal.

DECEMBER 1995

I tracked Michael down in England and insisted he take his belongings from my storage kingdom in Taos. I also suggested that we complete our relationship. He agreed to both requests.

Soon after his arrival, we processed the completion through improvisational movement. The group we were with gave us feedback as we performed our singles dance and our couple's dance. We also did several sacred pipe ceremonies.

Gazing eye to eye, however, we realized we did not want to be finished loving each other. I later told him he had been the first man who had joined me in the hard work of sorting through unresolved feelings and questions. We agreed to meet in six months to see if we still felt the potential for a loving relationship.

JUNE 1996

Love is an invitation to sacredness.

As I write these words, I am aware that a stream of channeling awaits my attention. I rest my pen against the page and record the information that comes through:

Love loves. It is not love which competes.
Love embraces. It is not love that fears.
Love multiplies. It is not love that subtracts.
Love cares. It is not love that judges.
Love ignites. It is not love that depresses.
I am love. I am love loving.

JULY 1996

Twelve women showed up for a Healing Hearts Grief Recovery workshop this evening. Their stories were heart wrenching: there was a mother whose son died four months ago of a drug overdose, a young woman whose mother committed suicide last year, another woman whose adopted daughter and granddaughter died in a fire four years ago, and a young woman whose first lover had recently died overseas. For such pain, a circle offers a safe container.

We told our stories as if sitting together were something we had always known. A veteran of grief, I encouraged the women to keep their hearts open, because I'd learned that souls depend on openheartedness. I reminded them that we owe it to ourselves and others to continue loving. Indeed, love is the healer.

JULY 1996

I miss Michael. I eat mussels and miss him. I walk on the beach and miss him. I go to bed and miss him. I went dancing last night and missed him.

This afternoon two tapes arrived from England; they were of Michael declaring his love for me over and over, and his wish for peace between us. While listening to them, I cried.

SEPTEMBER 1996

Could it be that with Michael living in England and me sitting here missing him, I am ready to embody what I express — namely, that talking is not enough? Action grounds talk. I know my future is with Michael. If my upcoming workshop in Vermont were not filled up, I would surprise him in England.

SEPTEMBER 1996

I record this conversation so as not to forget it. Michael's voice surprised me early this morning. He opened the phone conversation with: "I have a question for you, Rosalie. Will you marry me in this lifetime?"

"I'll consider that, Michael," I replied. "I know you have been committed to me since we met."

He then mentioned that he had visited a monastery in Greece last week, where he vowed to work on whatever stood in the way of healing his relationship with the feminine side of his consciousness. "I want to do whatever healing is necessary to be in relationship with you," he added.

I cry as I write. I feel as if I have been waiting eternally for him to say those words. Although we've often polarized along masculine and feminine lines, we seem to have surrendered to ALL of who we are. He is ready... Am I? Almost.

JUNE 1996

High heart — the place midway between the heart and the throat — is the seat of unconditional love. I'm wondering if jealousy, anger, even insecurity are perpetrated by those who are not able to reside in their high hearts.

"What is your capacity for living in your high heart?" That is the question I wish to ask myself and others. I do know joy is an expression of high heart.

It is becoming fruitless to try to determine whether my thoughts are mine or those of my guides, or even a combination of the two. I hereby relinquish my need to sort out who is in charge.

SEPTEMBER 1996

"Relationships are demanding," a friend told me this morning. "They require so much time and energy and angst. The price for kissing and cuddling is your life."

She said through teary eyes that she envied my independence and that marriage had cost her a great deal in terms of her creativity. I see the truth of that statement in her life. What aspects of human connectedness truly count?

SEPTEMBER 1996

While buying wine and chocolate after a long workday, I knew I wanted these comfort foods to stupefy my feelings. The cashier commented, "This is an evening to curl up with a good book." I silently answered her with, "I'd rather curl up with Michael."

MARCH 1997

It's strange that so many people speak of past lives but seldom mention future ones. Native Americans, on the other hand, regularly consult with future ancestors before making important decisions.

What links us to our future is love. Without its energizing power, we would remain forever in a mold formed by past hurts. Fueled by the energizing power of love, however, possibilities expand. When love beckons, destiny cheers.

NOVEMBER 1997

I was raised to believe in marriage. My grandmother married for life; my mother followed in her footsteps. I, on the other hand, cannot endure in a marriage that confines my spirit. Somewhere along the way, I have picked up the notion that love honors the soul, and consequently I've yearned to cocreate a soul-centered partnership.

As a result of choosing spirit over relationship, I have failed three times at being a wife. When I observe my friends' marriages, I notice women mothering men, and I marvel at how complicated their sex lives must be. As for me, although I have been married more years than I've been single, I have always felt entitled to a divorce.

Is it marriage per se that dampens passion and soul-seeking, or is it something else? Do I trust a man to honor both my vulnerability and my competence? I do believe that men and women can evolve together and that souls are for sharing. So maybe it is the inherent INEQUALITY in marriage that does not call to me.

FEBRUARY 1998

During a Candlemas ritual in Taos a few months ago, I publicly surrendered my resistance to success and to being in an intimate relationship. I acknowledged that healing within partnership was one of my life lessons. Is it the archetype of marriage that feels suffocating or have I created a reality based on a limited view of marriage? I am eager to see if success and healing within marriage are intertwined for me. Having surrendered my resistance, I expect to be happier.

Reflective Writing:

∾ **I LEARNED** how prevalent love has been in my life. Whether or not I was involved in a primary relationship, many of the values I have held about love pertain to my soul. I've also learned how vulnerable I feel in relationship. My fear showed up in many passages; yet yearning appeared, too, especially when I was less scared.

∾ **I RELEARNED** that I return to relationships for the opportunity to experience growth. Although I feel safe while alone, healing comes while I am in partnership.

∾ **I DISCOVERED** the compassion I feel for myself. How hard I have tried to get relationships "right"! In the process I have depended on the opinions of friends without considering that they, too, have been wounded.

∾ **I REDISCOVERED** love's exquisite sense of timing. Continually ready to hear the voice of love, I seemed unable to adopt its principles. In daring to trust a man once again, I experienced increased freedom.

∾ **I REGRET** that I was unable to embody love while in relationship. Still, I must share responsibility for the endings of these partnerships.

∾ **I APPRECIATE** my willingness to practice love in spite of failed relationships.

∾ **RIGHT NOW I FEEL** satisfied with the guises and disguises love has taken on in my life. I am grateful to those who played the role of shadow wisdom-teacher as I learned more about love.

∾ **AND I WILL** express gratitude daily for love's lessons. I will also remember my history and know that I am responsible for creating my future.

Invitation to Write

Did this bundling awaken thoughts about your own relationship to love? What's the most important question you now have about love? Who has taught you important love lessons? How has love come into your life? Can you track changes that occurred over time in your understanding of love?

If this topic intrigues you, now is the time to revisit your journals and begin piecing together your love history. Gather with love!

Following are a few quotations to help spark new thoughts:

"The heroic journey for women is taking the risk to love, day after day."

— Karen Signell

"Real intimacy is a journey into the unknown." — John Welwood

"Love has to be put into action, and that action is service." — Mother Teresa

"Let yourself be silently drawn to the pull of what you love." — Rumi

11

The Calling

FROM ALISON'S JOURNALS

In 1982 I left the school system, where I'd spent my entire professional career, and went to work as a full-time creativity consultant. I
loved focusing on creativity and innovation. Together with my business partner, I designed and delivered new programs to businesses
and organizations, including Fortune 50 companies. Traveling the
globe, we sat in the front of the plane.

In the spring of 1984 I stood on a brightly lit stage in Tokyo, acknowledging applause from hundreds of IBMers from the Asia Pacific
Rim after delivering a forty-five-minute presentation on right brain–left
brain thinking. I had the urge to pinch myself, for I had made more
money in those forty-five minutes than in my first two years of teaching children. It amused me that this presentation, aside from the
professional multimedia support we included, wasn't much different
from those I'd given to PTA groups for free!

Six months later I married my business partner. Our work took us
to Thailand, Bermuda, France, Nassau, and the Virgin Islands. For
more than a decade our business grew and we felt successful. Then
in late August of 1996 he narrowly missed suffering a potentially fatal
heart attack. While I led a workshop in New Jersey, he lay in a hospital
bed in Clearwater, Florida. Before I could get home to him, he'd had
the first of two surgeries that opened the clogged artery in the front
of his heart.

We looked at each other and said, "OK. This is a wake-up call. We have another chance." We agreed to question everything in our lives other than our relationship, which we both cherished. Metaphorically, we began unpacking our bags and examining what we'd been carrying around all those years. Only the endeavors that brought the greatest satisfaction or pleasure were to be repacked; everything else could go.

A month later I began rereading my journals. Although by then I knew I had been writing about Miss Perfect and other enduring motifs, I hadn't realized how long the goddess had been calling to me — telling me to change the nature of my work, to serve a higher purpose.

APRIL 20, 1990

I feel more and more compelled to go within. Our business is thriving, and many new opportunities will take us further. I'm as afraid of success as I was of becoming a bag lady when we started out! Most of all, I'm afraid I'll never write. I need time to think...to stay connected to purpose beyond profit. Time to be alone and quiet. How do I balance my professional life with this irrational longing?

AUGUST 25, 1990

I've been reading Natalie Goldberg's *Writing Down the Bones*. She refers to the saying "Trust in what you love, continue to do it and it will take you where you need to go." Then she writes: "And don't worry too much about security. You will have a security money can never bring you once you begin to do what your heart calls you to do. How many of us with our big salaries are actually that secure anyway?"

Bless you, Natalie, for the reminder. Now I want to BELIEVE all that and LIVE it, not just stare at it.

OCTOBER 19, 1990

Disquieted. No logical reason to feel so unsettled and off center. I ask my wiser self (WS) to tell me what it knows.

WS: I'll tell you...You forgot your promise.

ME: What promise?

WS: You even forgot what your promise was?

ME: Yes. Pretty ironic, huh?

WS: To remember who...

ME: Yes, now I recall — to remember who I am. I hurry about with so much to do that it's getting harder and harder to think about what gives me energy and courage. Do remembering who I am and being a successful businesswoman contradict each other? I have exactly what I thought I wanted ten years ago. Why isn't it enough?

WS: Because you want to write. Because you must work from your heart.

JUNE 22, 1992

I find myself more interested in "heart stirring" than brainstorming. I don't want to write an academic book about creativity; I want to write about creativity of the heart. I got into this creativity business wanting to be smarter, get better ideas. I loved using the "tricks of the trade" to invent things. I loved new ideas. Now it's not much fun. I'm getting bored. It doesn't stir my heart or feed my soul. More and more I ask, "Creativity in service of what?" Creativity for its own sake is no longer enough.

OCTOBER 26, 1993

Home again, after an intense trip north to facilitate a new product development session. It went well, but why am I not happy with all the positive feedback? Because we have enough household cleaners! I'm tired of "widget creativity." I know that product development work simply gets us in the door to introduce people to creativity; yet the "reframing" isn't working as well as it once did. I am feeling a sense of urgency about the well-being of our planet. I fear we'll "extinct" ourselves with our new products before we wake up!

What if we put as much time, energy, and money into inventing new ways to live together as we do new products to consume? Such work would truly be worthy.

OCTOBER 29, 1993

This morning by the pool I was rereading some of Deena Metzger's *Writing for Your Life*. I'm drawn to her stories. I'll take good stories over theory any day, especially women's stories.

Why? Because women's stories affirm and clarify. I connect with them, seeing my own life reflected in theirs, seeing their journeys mirrored in mine. They help me understand, give me courage and hope and a vision of spiraling to a new awareness. Always, I am diving down to reclaim another part of myself first glimpsed in another's life.

Certain questions must be asked again and again, Deena suggests, such as WHAT IS IT YOU WANT TO KNOW? I want to know more of the great mystery, of God in hiding. Where is he hiding? Where does she hide? Goddess, spirit that calls, hounds of heaven —where are they and what do they want of me? I of them?

They hide in the details of everyday life. Inside laughter, inside a glistening tear that wells up unbidden and overflows as certainly as my foolish need to hold it back.

I want from *God/Goddess*, Holy Spirit, Great Mystery, All That Is to understand my place and purpose in this vast universe. I long to be of service on this lovely, defiled, and troubled planet. I must use my creativity in service of something beyond myself. I want to live from the heart and dwell in peace. I want to shed the shell that confines.

FEBRUARY 1996 (A FEW WEEKS AFTER MY MOTHER'S DEATH)

In the middle of yesterday's entry about exhaustion so deep I couldn't think, frustration over taking care of the final details of Mom's estate, and the last errand I would ever run for her — going to the cemetery to pay for interning her ashes — I found this sentence: "I don't care about creativity divorced from spirit."

The morning before, I recorded a dream. I'd had a baby. Although I didn't remember the birth, suddenly I was holding this perfect little baby without knowing its gender or name, only that it was mine. This tells me something's been born fully formed and ready to grow. I need only discover more about it.

Today, I'm toying with the idea of "Creating a Life" as a theme for our work — bringing in a search for balance that triggers the search for meaning. More and more people in our workshops raise issues related to these two life themes.

(Note: Portions of this entry foreshadow the new direction our work took in 1998, when we wrote a career discovery field guide and designed workshops to help people find out who they are and what they're here to do. Our work is still about creativity, but the application has shifted from "technology for creating ideas that work" to "principles for creating a life that works.")

JUNE 27, 1996 (AT THE CREATIVE PROBLEM SOLVING INSTITUTE [CPSI])

I am almost afraid to listen to the voice in the wind — the voice that whispers to me, telling me how bored I am with my work. There's not enough heart space; there's a hole only spirit can fill. I am lonely for my soul. Is it only here in this circle of writers that I create space for what I truly love?

I am tired of overheads and flip charts. I much prefer to teach while sitting on the ground.

JUNE 29, 1996 (A DREAM: THE BLACK MADONNA)

I am about to hold a workshop in a house we've just bought. It's older and huge, with lots of rooms and separate outbuildings. There's even a restaurant where people can gather. Parts of the house have not yet been renovated. A new client organization is there for a Creative Business Teams workshop. I know that if this one goes well there will be more to come. A big contract's at stake.

I'm with workshop participants in a old English tavernlike room of the house where everyone's relaxing before dinner. Rosalie's there and begins channeling in Celtic. (In reality I have no idea what the language sounds like, but in the dream I know that's what she's speaking.) Her voice is deep and throaty, her eyes blazing. She's radiating intensely assertive, determined energy. I try to catch her attention to tell her to stop. Wrong audience, Rosalie! These businesspeople are really straight. Not here, PLEASE! She goes on, oblivious to me.

A woman facing her watches intently and then answers in Celtic. Rosalie listens thoughtfully while this woman speaks to her. I look around the group apologetically. "This isn't part of the workshop," I say to a woman seated beside me. She replies, "Well, she said you hadn't gotten it yet!" Her words sting — I feel betrayed, hurt, and confused. My soul sister would never hold me in such disregard. Is Rosalie possessed? What's going on here?

I step out onto a large stone terrace, where I see my friend Gus. "Damn it, Gus! I've got an important new client here and Rosalie's down there channeling in Celtic. If I lose this client, I'm going to be really pissed off! What the hell is going on?" He gives me an impish, whimsical smile and winks at me.

Waking, I felt intrigued but uneasy. Who was Rosalie in this dream? I relaxed and drifted back into the imagery. As my body began to feel heavy, I heard a voice: "She speaks for the Black Madonna."

I know I need to read Marion Woodman's new book, *Dancing in the Flames: The Dark Goddess in the Transformation of Consciousness.* I know I'm being asked to connect with feminine wisdom. The woman in the dream who answered Rosalie in Celtic tells me that the business world can hear and respond to the voice of the goddess. The goddess herself tells me she's determined and I must listen. I will buy Marion Woodman's book today and show the goddess I got it!

SEPTEMBER 12, 1996

I'll turn sixty in this journal. Around that time Ted will finish getting his heart opened up, and we'll have an even clearer picture of what we want. I have read that sixty begins the active phase of old age. In many ways I know this is true — not old and breaking down, but old and breaking through.

Disengaging from frenzy, I feel myself becoming solitary, still, reflective. Rather than dive into a current bestseller, I'd sooner reread a cherished old book, distilling what I can from it. I'd ask myself questions like why it called to me the first time and how it speaks to me now. I'd notice what I underlined then and what I underline now.

I relish this quiet pace. Instead of running through airports, we walk the beach in the late afternoon talking about heart and soul health, what we want to create in the years to come, the legacy we hope to leave. I'm most interested in questions that lead to purpose: first the *WHY*, then the *HOW*.

JUNE 28, 1997 (AT CPSI'S THE WRITING PLACE)

I want to remember:

  ∿ Feeling centered, confident, focused, surefooted, clearheaded, and openhearted

∾ How good my writing is becoming after years of scribbling

∾ The beauty of this community we've created under the willow trees

∾ Sitting here by the lake, caressed by Buffalo breezes, content in the morning and open to the day

SEPTEMBER 27, 1997 (ON A FLIGHT HOME FROM PORTLAND, MAINE)

Amid eyes tearing with gratitude, I must state at last: *I AM A WRITER.* I want this writer's life for the rest of my life. Even if it means never again having the financial success I've enjoyed. Even if this is my last first-class flight.

APRIL 1, 1998 (A DREAM: HANGIN' WITH CHARLES KURALT)

Last night I dreamed I spent a day with author Charles Kuralt. I walk into his home unexpected, but welcomed. Decorated throughout in shades of gray, it evokes a masculine sense of streamlined simplicity.

We talk about writing, how he shaped his books, the joy of working at what we love. While telling him how my work has changed, I lie on the couch with my head in his lap as if we've been friends for a lifetime. When I leave, he hugs and kisses me — nothing sexual, just with warmth and understanding. Only as I walk away do I realize who he is and that he's now dead. "That can't be!" I think, but when I turn around, he's gone and his house has vanished.

Then I am standing on the thick, soft carpet of a meeting room furnished with rich wooden window seats and built-in tables lining the walls. Pillows provide the only seating. As images of workshops led by people I admire flash through my mind, I wonder, "Is this place Esalen?" I see myself teaching in this room. It has a sacred quality to it.

Who was Charles Kuralt? A writer who used simple words to say profound things. The author of books that poetically describe everyday life yet never lapse into sentimentality. A soulful, grounded nature lover who quit being a war correspondent in favor of telling stories about common people. A devourer of sensual pleasures — good food, fine wines. Although he did not marry well, I've often thought he'd make a good friend to a woman. He left a job that no longer served him to spend his final twelve months of life revisiting favorite places. Years ago I chose him as the man I'd most like to be marooned on a desert island with, because of his big heart and deep soul.

Why did he come to me in a dream? To accept me as a colleague, a fellow writer. In addition, he helped me feel relaxed and comfortable rather than worried as usual about finishing this or beginning that. His appearance suggests that I need to take time to just be; that I, like him, am approaching a decision to change the arena in which I ply my craft; that it is best not to wait to do the things I love, to live the dreams I envision.

Why the learning room? First I was tempted to write, "I wish to teach only in such a sacred space," but I immediately spotted the trap: such a space can be ANYWHERE I happen to be working with the sacred.

JUNE 6, 1998

I'm reading Gregg Levoy's *Callings: Finding and Following an Authentic Life.* I'm drawn to it because in rereading my journals I've seen that my yearning to write surfaced eons ago. At first, my muse only whispered her call. Then her voice grew progressively louder until she seemed to be shouting at me! It took a sorrow-filled year marked by mother loss, followed by Ted's close brush with death, to wake me up.

Gregg writes, too, about tapping into the underground stream of the unconscious to bring hidden longings to the surface. Writing in my journal has helped me tap into the deep well of whispers fed by these subterranean springs. Harvesting my journals has taught me how to bring back seedlings of understanding, not yet knowing how they will fit into my life but ready to see what they want to become. Now I understand that writing has not only provided a conduit for the whispers but was part of what I longed for. For years I described myself as a consultant who sometimes writes; now I see myself as a writer who sometimes consults.

I never want to give up teaching completely— I've been a teacher all my life. And helping people develop their creativity will always be part of what I teach. Yet never again will I allow myself to get so distracted that I fail to hear my muse's whispers.

Reflective Writing:

❧ **I LEARNED** that being a writer has long been part of who I am.

❧ **I RELEARNED** that writing in my journal keeps me true to myself.

❧ **I DISCOVERED** that the deep longing I've felt is sacred and will persist despite new business contracts and other exciting projects. I want to contribute more than I take.

❧ **I REDISCOVERED** that my aversion to hurry sickness is part of my calling to write.

❧ **I REGRET** that I didn't take my writing more seriously years ago.

❧ **I APPRECIATE** the progress I've made on a quest that each step of the way seemed to move so slowly. And I must honor my current desire to ask questions, listen for responses, and find my own answers.

❧ **RIGHT NOW I FEEL** a desire to live my life "on purpose."

❧ **AND I WILL** trade in my hectic, people-packed existence for the quiet needed for writing.

Invitation to Write

What signs of "calling" have you experienced? When did you first hear them? What did you do about them? Which callings went unanswered? Which ones did you recognize and act on? Which ones captured your attention for a while and then faded? Why did they die out — did you outgrow them or deny them? What might be calling you now?

A few quotes worth writing from:

"Women must turn to one another for stories; they must share the stories of their lives and their hopes and their unacceptable fantasies." — Carolyn Heilbrun

"Attentive waiting is an aspect of both monasticism and a writer's life."
— Kathleen Norris

"To work is to rearrange, invent, make possible, invite the dance of the atoms, the music of the fields of energy. Work is full of surprise and wonder."
— Matthew Fox

"Successful writers are not the ones who write the best sentences. They are the ones who keep writing."
— Bonnie Friedman

12

Transitions

FROM ROSALIE'S JOURNALS

I carefully recorded my major transitions, each of which formed not only openings but also opportunities to stop pretending. Sometimes I wrote about an integrating insight; other times I simply recorded the external experience. Weeding out all these entries helped me see that the words I wrote in the early 1980s, when I was in my mid-thirties, already showed signs of sprouting wisdom roots. As I continued to season, they grew into the mature root system that now supports me.

JANUARY 1978

Out of a sense of awe, I am reluctant to write about an experience I had today. Was it a dream or a visitation? An illusion, perhaps?

A woman dressed in a monk's robe approached and beckoned me to follow her, unaware that I was embedded in the cocoon of a gestating butterfly. The robed lady invited me to fly with her, but I heard voices warning, "It's too soon." Sensing that I must join her despite my apprehension, I relaxed, shape-shifted into human form, expanded, and took flight. The gentle lady extended her hands, motioning me to follow her. As she pointed out galaxies and planets, as well as scenes on the earth, I immediately understood how multidimensional human nature is.

Suddenly, the woman's face, which radiated love, beauty, and wisdom, transformed into the body of Christ. Simultaneously, my body filled with light. As he reached out his hands toward me, I recognized them from a dream I had years ago. "Why me?" I asked fearfully.

Showered by his recognition of my light, I realized I had agreed to touch people with my hands. Furthermore, I understood that my hands were an extension of my healing heart. I then began a healing dance, after which Jesus placed in my hands a wandlike figure that reminded me of an agreement I had made to inspire hope in others.

How do I begin to make sense of this experience? I'm afraid that if I shared it with friends I might be locked up! For now, it is enough to chronicle it here. I feel as if I am being courted by the sacred.

(Note: Now, twenty years later, I am living this vision. Healing is part of my work, and daily I invoke the sacred. How grateful I am to have a record of my call to this spirit-centered life!)

JUNE 1981 (ON THE EVENING OF MY SEPARATION)

As I begin a new life, it is important to notice what I am bringing forward in addition to what I am leaving behind.

APRIL 1985

Communication with my guides punctuates my life. Recognizing the signals of a message, I surrender to being a cosmic secretary:

> *You will experience more vitality as you commit yourself to your soul's path. It has been important to read your journals once more, noting and appreciating your beginnings. Your transitions have not been easy, but they have all been necessary. Remember there are no endings — only more and more ways of deepening your understanding and connecting with other realms of experience.*

JANUARY 1991

The friends attending my naming ritual enfolded me in hugs. I dressed for the celebration in a maroon skirt and handmade velvet vest of many colors. My feet were bare. Everyone brought a special dish and a musical instrument. As for the three-layered chocolate cake, circling its top and sides was the affirmation "Woman giving birth to herself."

At first I was shy, because nobody in my family of origin honored beginnings or endings, much less understood the importance of rituals. Indeed, Kelli-Lynne, at sixteen, was the only family member present. Aloud to my friends, I confessed I was feeling awkward, which brought relief.

As we sat in a candle-lit circle, I was invited to tell the story of my spiritual name. In response I shared the journey into dreamtime I had taken to request a name that would remind me of my spiritual path, and subsequently announced my commitment to live my life accordingly. I felt as if I had been a storyteller forever.

After finishing the tale, I was asked to enter the circle and dance my name. Unprepared for a center-stage performance, the little girl inside me felt awkward. Pushed to the center, however, I moved without self-consciousness to the natural rhythms of my name. Friends mirrored my movements.

Then someone began to drum, and the steady beat drew me into the cells of my body, where my name felt deeply grounded. Without warning, thirty friends encircled me, chanting, "Rosalie Deer Heart" over and over again. As I merged with the music, my sense of time and space disappeared, giving way to a name that spanned all dimensions.

Then there was silence. Standing in the center of the circle, with tears of celebration and love flowing from my eyes, I vowed to keep the name Rosalie Deer Heart forever: "I wish to be cremated with this name," I said solemnly. Looking from one person to the next, I spoke my name aloud, whereupon each person in turn addressed me by my spiritual name. Before I knew what had happened, my friends had formed two parallel lines and I was being propelled through the birth tunnel. Hugs and shouts of welcome greeted my emergence as Rosalie Deer Heart.

MAY 1991

I have retreated to a convent five miles from the town I grew up in. Audrey, my spiritual mother, and I are staying here for thirty-six uninterrupted hours. Although in this lifetime I have been a Protestant, being surrounded by nuns feels familiar to my soul.

During tonight's simple meat-and-potatoes supper, one of the sisters, hearing of my forthcoming move to New Mexico, asked, "Are you going there as a missionary?"

Clearly, she had assumed that I, too, was a sister. "No," I answered, "as a person."

"Why New Mexico?" another nun asked.

Before I could answer, someone else chimed in with, "Why now?"

Without thinking, I replied, "Because that is where God wants me to be." I felt the ring of truth in my answer.

"How long will you be living there?" asked a sister seated at the other end of the long table.

"I don't know. God hasn't told me that part yet. All I know is that once I heard the call to live there, I decided to follow it."

Sister Anita, seated beside me, reached for my hand and said softly, "It must be hard to leave your friends, your career, and the only life you have known."

"Yes," I replied, almost in a whisper, "yet I have faith that all will unfold in perfect order."

"Bless you, Deer Heart," said a sister who had not yet joined in the conversation.

"Thank you," I said softly. "I would be honored if you'd each pray for me while I am gone."

Tears spilled down my face. All I could see in response to my request were ten heads nodding.

AUGUST 1991

My new neighbor Jenna explained that her two years of living 7,500 feet above sea level on northern New Mexico's El Salto Mountain have been a time of reaching out. I listened to her stories with fascination, because my experience feels so different.

I am learning to cherish each day without looking to the future or bemoaning the past. I have more time alone than ever before. Gone are the methods I once used to mark my life: schedules, earning an income by seeing enough psychotherapy clients, or by teaching a sufficient number of courses. Working no longer adds to my self-esteem. Instead, my days are marked by pleasure, and the satisfaction I derive is deep and lasting.

Walking, coming upon a ripening rose, beholding the sensuous profile of the surrounding mountains, watching dogs romp and the play of light on the leaves all add to my pleasure. As I let go of habits adopted long ago, the emptying that moves within me feels the way clothes hung outside might feel as the wind caresses their wrinkles.

SEPTEMBER 1992

I awoke this morning feeling safe. Connecting to my soul is all that matters to me now.

OCTOBER 1992

At breakfast, friends spoke of a woman who recently discovered she has only six months to live. We discussed what we would do upon learning that we were living on limited time. Several women said they would stuff their lives with all the experiences they had not yet had. When it was my turn to speak, I said I would use the time remaining to erase traces of fear from my energy field.

To me, death feels more like a celebration than a deprivation. No doubt, this perception is based on Mike's ongoing presence in my life. Although he has been dead for fifteen years, he remains accessible to me.

OCTOBER 1992

Today I drove to Abiquiu, land of the red cliffs that Georgia O'Keeffe portrayed on many of her canvases. Since the vibrations on El Salto Mountain are intense and demanding, I was ready for gentleness — as was my friend Anne, who had flown in from Maine while recovering from major surgery. And secretly, I suspected that the soft, feminine energies of Abiquiu had a gift for me.

Upon our arrival, we looked to nature for direction. Right away, I spied a huge mound of pink alabaster similar to rocks I had seen in Egypt, and I decided to meditate beside it. Suddenly, energies akin to those in Cairo's Third Pyramid surrounded me, and I felt myself moving into another dimension. While leaning against a bowl-shaped stone, I announced my readiness to learn more. Immediately, I felt as if I were being cradled and rocked in preparation for a visit to a parallel lifetime. I breathed softly, holding a piece of the alabaster in my left hand to ground myself.

In the lifetime I entered, my birth was eagerly awaited. From my first breath on, I was in training to be a healer. Everyone in the village participated in my education. At a young age, however, I rejected the relative ease of this lifetime in favor of grappling with the challenges inherent in my present one. I could see that I had chosen to be born into a family and a world that was unconscious of my soul's purpose.

I smiled and heard myself saying, "You really did it this time, Rosalie." As the sun caressed my face, I gave myself over to the once familiar, easy ways of knowing, and accepted as my motto "Struggle no longer." A dozen swifts encircled me, appearing as if from nowhere as a sign of freedom and ease. I thanked them for their visit and vowed to reclaim my heritage as a healer.

MAY 1992

Kelli-Lynne's forthcoming graduation from high school stirs up my vulnerability. I did not graduate from high school, because I was pregnant. Then Mike died while in ninth grade. Since Kelli-Lynne is the first child in my branch of the family to graduate, I had been fantasizing about a big family celebration. In reality, I will be the only family member celebrating with her, and I want to FEEL THIS PASSAGE.

Although Kelli-Lynne's senior year of high school has been gentle for us, we played the parts of angry mother and misunderstood teenager stunningly during her sophomore and junior years. Moving to New Mexico bonded us — in part, because we knew no one else here. Another reason we deepened our connection is that I've plunged into this last opportunity to engage in full-time mothering. But now that my career as a mother is almost over, I do not feel ready to graduate. I yearn to hear women's stories about their daughters leaving home. Yes, grief visits once more.

SEPTEMBER 1994

At last I have settled into my home in San Cristobal, New Mexico. After forsaking my short-sleeved shirt and bra, figuring that would be enough, I stripped off my shorts and panties so I could be closer to the earth.

I used to think my urge to be naked arose out of rebellion against family and cultural values. I've since decided that nakedness is one way I have of honoring my relationship with the earth. When I am without clothes, no boundaries exist between my body and the moss, flowers, trees, and rocks — or between me and the cool waters of a stream, and the sun as it kisses me dry.

The fast-moving, gurgling river heightens my senses — so much so that I smile, remembering that several of Aphrodite's rendezvous pools in Cyprus are now national landmarks. The wind, too, is present. The cool breeze caressing the leaves of the trees reminds me that I am in a place of peace. The only interruptions have been a few curious flies landing on my fingers as they glide across these pages.

Divine leisure beckons. I respond with a deep yawn, realizing that this is what the practice of "being present" is all about. Yes, one must be present until "presence" becomes the practice. When I create opportunities to be present for the Earth Mother, I feel closer to the poetry of my soul. Resting my pen against my thigh, I take in the deliciousness of nature. Even the need to say yes has disappeared.

JULY 1995

Over the weekend, Mary Rae and I hatched a business—a card company we intend to call Ripe Tomatoes. My grandmother is embarrassed that one of the cards features a black-and-white photograph of me seated nude on a large rock, about to launch myself into the Pemaquid River. (Mary Rae's husband Don snapped the picture, and I was the last to know of it.) The caption on the card reads, "Without pretense, I am menopausal."

The mission of our card company is to celebrate women's rites of passage. Designing the cards itself fulfills this purpose. During the weekend, for instance, we drew the images and conjured up the text in between swimming nude in the soft, brown waters of the river. I love swimming through bouquets of water lilies and maneuvering my body so the blossoms cover my breasts.

Yesterday, Mary Rae and I finalized the card designs, then I took the prototypes to be duplicated. We are delighted to be going public with menopause, one of women's secret passages — more secret than sex. Perhaps these cards will help air the critical questions: How do we prepare, welcome, and encourage other women as they come of age? Where are the stories of those who had an easy time of this transition? What losses do women experience around menopause? What are the gains?

AUGUST 1995

Last month I was bitten by a brown recluse — a poisonous spider. The toxins continue to travel through my bloodstream. To my mind, I have been initiated into the spider lodge!

Looking back with the detachment that only time provides, I appreciate the exposure I've had to many strains of spider teaching. I come from strong New England stock that breeds women who, like the spider, make due. No matter what the challenge — weather, relationship, career, motherhood — I tend to be self-sufficient and strong.

This particular spider bit me at night, although I did not feel its sting until waking in the morning. A small circle of raised red skin on my left arm announced the attack. Then as the day progressed, I felt increasingly sluggish and feverish, all the while chiding myself for acting like a wimp. Aspirin brought no relief; soothing teas did not help; meditation was impossible. For two weeks I continued to swim and belly dance until my left shoulder seemed to weigh as much as the rest of my body.

A visit to the local homeopath was in order. It was he who informed me that the culprit was a brown recluse spider—whose toxins, he added, are more deadly than a tarantula's or a black widow's. He stated that movement must be restricted to keep the venom contained, to prevent the acids from entering my bloodstream and causing paralysis.

During the next forty-eight hours, I vacillated between living and dying, staying with neither one. I then began reviewing my life, revisiting, among other incidents, three in which I was unable to tell myself, "Well done!" Clarity and sadness engulfed me as I realized how inauthentic my behavior had been in these instances. After voicing my regrets, I understood that I could CHOOSE between living and dying. This must have been the signal I had been waiting for! Right away, I chose to return to my body and seize upon the opportunity to meet my three shadow teachers with integrity. I felt both sobered and excited about the chance to say, "Well done!" the second time around.

When I at last returned to consciousness, my body was hot and achy. All the same, I declared my resolve to weave in the three dissonant strands of my "web." From that day forth, I have carried not only the spider's medicine and its ability to see through to creation, but also the understanding of what "Well done!" means to my soul.

NOVEMBER 1996

With the rising sun at my back, I reflect on Kelli-Lynne, who is now an older version of the child I knew. She is attentive to her fiancé, David, frequently asking if he is OK, especially when he is quiet. They touch often, and she usually calls him "honey."

Yesterday morning Kelli-Lynne disappeared into the bedroom and, after several minutes, asked me to join her. There she stood in the middle of the room dressed as a bride! The train of her gown was long, making it hard for her to walk. "Do you like it, Mom?" she asked. "You don't think it's too loose? I'm going to have to pin the bra straps because the weight of the dress pulls them down. How do we iron it?"

Amid this flurry of questions I could only marvel at how gorgeous she looked. A moment later I was beset by questions of my own: Why is she playing "dress up" so early in the day? Where has the time gone? Only yesterday she was rebelling against homework and refusing to shower, and here she is trying on her wedding gown!

Later in the day, I asked David what he was going to call me when they were married, and he said, without a second's delay, "Mom." It has been forever since a boy has called me Mom.

JULY 1997

This summer in Maine I feel an uncustomary vigilance in my bones. The headlines in the local paper the day I arrived reported a triple murder; the dead men, including the accused murderer, were in their early twenties. Two days later, two young adults who had beaten a fifty-nine-year-old woman to death in a neighboring town were apprehended in Florida. That evening the local paper appealed for information about a woman who had been pregnant and now was not. The partially decomposed body of an infant was eventually discovered wrapped in a garbage bag a few miles from my home.

In the past, I've found seeds of promise in tragedy. Today, I do not. I crave meaning and connection, not the stark consequences of alienation. I have been introduced to the shadow side of spirit, and I grieve.

Reflective Writing:

- ∾ **I LEARNED** that what served as transitions in my thirties became initiations in my forties and fifties, many of which I consciously chose to undergo.

- ∾ **I RELEARNED** how much I've relied on my intuition and how often I have come home to my body's wisdom.

- ∾ **I DISCOVERED** that a myriad of feelings have accompanied my life changes. Books became less and less authoritative; experts, too, disappeared as I risked trusting the integrity of my own experiences.

- ∾ **I REDISCOVERED** many ways in which my body has alerted me to transitions. At times, only a few precious days passed between voicing a question about initiation and undergoing the experience of it. Synchronicity was stalking me, and I took notice.

- ∾ **I REGRET** how alone I felt during most of my transitions.

- ∾ **I APPRECIATE** the courage and stamina I was able to muster in times of risk. In each instance of facing the unknown, I risked more, my mind expanded, and my heart cheered. It is as though I carried a banner reading: I'm Changing My Consciousness. Please Do Not Disturb.

- ∾ **RIGHT NOW I FEEL** a desire to let friends know of my questions instead of only the answers I have already arrived at.

- ∾ **AND I WILL** ask close friends for support.

🌸 Invitation to Write

How do you define *transition*? How do you know if you are in the midst of one? What lessons have transitions brought you? If you were offered one hour to speak to your grandchildren about transitions in your life, what would you say? What do your dreams tell you about transitions?

Returning to your journals with your magical butterfly net in hand, snare your times of transition, then write about them. Here are quotations to spur you on:

"Something is ending when its energy dwindles." — Christina Baldwin

"There is nothing like returning to a place that is unchanged to see how you have altered." — Nelson Mandela

"There are moments when we experience self-evolution, when the structure of who we are is changed by choice or circumstance." — Ann Linnea

"We must be willing to get rid of the life we have planned, so as to have the life that is awaiting us." — Joseph Campbell

13

Solitude

FROM ALISON'S JOURNALS

In the early 1990s I started to write entries about my growing need for solitude and my aversion to the hurry sickness I felt in my life, some of which is described in chapter 11. I longed to withdraw from the busy pace I'd lived for so many years that simultaneous processing of multiple tasks had become my way of life. I sensed a growing need for focused, quiet reflection. At first, I fretted that I might be getting old, losing my edge. Then I realized I'd stepped onto a new growth spiral that was turning me inward to reclaim forgotten parts of myself and find my own voice.

MARCH 24, 1991

A poem came to me through the ethers this morning and flowed unsought onto a fresh sheet of paper. While writing it, I felt my body lighten, my breathing deepen, and my neck relax. The words hinted at a richer reality beyond the rush of daily life. I called the poem "Something More." I don't consider it "good" poetry; I'm more interested in where it came from, unexpected and full-blown as I sat alone by the pool.

I wonder what other poems might come to me if I were to take the time to sit and listen. I worry that I'll be too busy darting about to find out what "something more" may actually be.

JANUARY 3, 1992

The house is quiet. Christmas has come and gone. Our kids have all returned to their own lives. Only the tree remains, and I luxuriate in this quiet morning, enjoying its light and savoring my solitude. It's wonderful to gather the family together for the holidays. It's also wonderful to rest here alone, gathering myself together before the new year picks up speed.

I remember the first time I longed for solitude: I was a twenty-two-year-old college student, wife, and mother. One evening after dinner, I left my husband and sleeping three-year-old daughter and walked to a friend's house to share a beer. As I reached the handle of Ann's back porch screen door, I suddenly saw myself ALONE in a mountain cabin, away from husband and child, with time to ponder who I really was. I felt a deep longing for me. Within seconds, my mind flashed back to a vivid memory of myself as a girl lying alone on a soft patch of grass in our church yard down the block. I watched puffy clouds drift overhead while my imaginary stallion grazed nearby. How I hoped no other kids would come and disturb my delicious aloneness or frighten my horse away! I think I was eight.

Then I opened the door and stepped into Ann's kitchen. I can't remember what we talked about that night, but I've never forgotten my moment of longing.

JUNE 2, 1992 (IN THE BACK OF A ROOM IN WHICH WORKSHOP PARTICIPANTS ARE DRAWING QUIETLY, EXPLORING THE RIGHT SIDE OF THEIR BRAINS)

Who is this woman I sense within? She is the artist — the unspoiled core of every person — who has been so choked by schooling, training, and social conditioning that early on she began shriveling up and fading into oblivion. The artist never fully succumbs, however. At times she will awaken, stirred, perhaps, by the wild beauty of nature. Brought back to life, she will instantly remind us that we stand in the presence of a primal mystery. She renews the spirit and lets us know that life is a miraculous gift longing for expression. But run too fast and she'll continue to slumber within, whereupon neither of us will awaken to the mystery.

I long for stretches of time to ponder the many questions I cannot answer, as well as those I answer one way today and another tomorrow. I yearn to spend days silently contemplating the enigmas that swirl about within me, circling back repeatedly for new answers, each of which builds on those that came before. Such quests call for quiet time.

OCTOBER 1, 1993

My brain has shut down. I don't want to do anything or think about anything; I only want to BE. I'm not depressed, just overwhelmed and closing down. It's time to replenish the spirit, to let go of agendas for a little while.

These interludes scare me. I worry that I won't be able to stay fully engaged in our business. I wonder if I'm selfishly letting Ted down when I withdraw. Even though he understands my need for time alone, I feel a conflict between "should be more productive" and needing to know I'm alive and present in the world.

I feel worn out by a life that moves too fast. For forty years I've been "on call" and now I want breathing room.

OCTOBER 2, 1993

Cool morning. Doves call to one another. My tiredness lifts, as does my sense of distractedness. Just saying, "Enough!" and coming out here by the pool to read and write restores my balance. While moving through this overscheduled month, I must remember to take time alone — because if I don't, I may endanger body, mind, and spirit.

OCTOBER 6, 1993

As soon as I can slow down enough, I want to write about hurry sickness. It's endemic in our lives. Our sense of meaning and purpose unravels each time we rush to catch a plane set to depart with or without us, and each time we race to complete an agenda. Driven by schedules, I'm afraid I'll catch all the planes, meet all the deadlines, and lose my soul in the process.

Author Larry Dossey, MD, says that what ails one of us ails us all and what heals one of us heals us all. Certainly, our politico-economic system no longer serves, but how might the dynamics be changed without further disrupting people's lives? Is there a tolerable level of chaos that would allow for the evolution of a new order?

There's a sickness afoot in the land. The infection erupts in pustules of violence — battered children, bludgeoned tourists, road rage exploding into murder because someone cut off an angry armed driver. Accounts of such phenomena fill the daily news reports, yet we're too numb to weep or cry aloud in outrage. Instead, we make sick jokes.

Better ways already exist — such as learning to speak and listen from the heart, and to honor the sacred spirit within each person. That's what I will try to do with today's workshop participants.

AFTER THE WORKSHOP...

During periodic pauses in the guided imagery I led, I began PRAYING! Welling up from a quiet, centered place inside me came a prayer for the clarity and wisdom to know when my instinct to withdraw into contemplation serves the highest good — for me, the people I care for, and the work I'm committed to — and when it degenerates into self-centered, whiny "chicken-shit stuff." I smiled at the prayerful vulgarity, aware that it was rising from the heart prayer and that Great Spirit and the beings that sometimes guide me would know that and accept it.

I cut my teeth on the work ethic. Even so, I know that productivity doesn't require dipping your bucket dry and fraying your nervous system until it turns on you and fire alarms go off at the slightest provocation. How ironic it would be to discover that all this activity yields disease and premature death instead of freedom to work with a calm mind and steady heart toward a chosen dream!

How can I tell the difference between Work and work? A voice I heard midway through the prayer said, "This is how — you go inside and listen. You listen all the time, not just when the alarms go off."

We believe we can't afford to slow down. We believe we'll never have enough. We worry and fret about the damnedest things, trapping ourselves in indecisiveness while so many issues demand our attention that we can hardly bear to think about them. That's how I've been living lately. So what can I do about it? The answer, the little voice whispered, is to love myself more and take better care of me. I suspect this prescription applies to others as well.

JANUARY 17, 1994

I've been reading Cathleen Roundtree's *Women Turning 50*. So many of the accomplished women she interviewed for the book spoke of the need for solitude to cope with the fast-paced environment they live in — not because they can't cope, but because they need solitude to reflect, assimilate, and gain wise perspectives.

JULY 1, 1995

I relish Judith Duerk's book, *I Sit Listening to the Wind*. A few nights ago, after a bout of exhaustion so deep it frightened me, I read a page to Ted. A few lines into it, I burst into tears. Judith's words touched a longing for stillness so acute it ached. These words, in particular, teach me the lesson demanding to be learned: "As I allow myself to mature, an awareness comes of a slender ribbon of energy, no longer robust as in my youth. I learn to tend it carefully… avoid excess, exercise restraint. To use my strength ever more sacramentally, for I suffer more each time I use it in service to old distractions."

I used to be able to overextend myself for months, with no discernible effects. Now it takes days to recover from an energy binge. I must expend my precious energy carefully, using it only to work toward what truly matters, and not fret over the rest. A few stolen moments of solitude no longer serve; to hear the whispers of my deeper self, I must have them in large and regular doses!

JANUARY 5, 1996

Activist writer and poet Alice Walker craves solitude. As she put it in a *New Age Journal* (November/December 1993) interview: "It's so important to unclutter the brain, the mind. This society is so full of junk that for me, creativity is greatly impeded just by the chatter of all those things and the visual clutter of life. So I need to be able to see great distances, clear to the horizon for one thing, and also have a lot of time that is quiet and pure, in which there is no noise or bills to pay. It's just very important to have a space that is really, really clear for whatever is trying to come."

I know what you mean, Alice. I long for huge spaces of time for playing around with words. As for now, I must grab moments when they come, writing in snatched intervals.

Madeleine L'Engle's journals reflect a similar process. She writes in the midst of domestic life — raising children, tending to others' children, caring for her elderly mother in her last days, and sitting beside her dying husband. Late at night I've been reading her journals, and appreciating how much she's helped me live this sad passage.

Thank you, Madeleine, for keeping me company during these dark winter nights. Your courage steels mine. Your claiming of quiet moments for yourself, no matter what family chaos swirls around you, inspires me. You kept writing and reminding me I could, too. That's a great gift, for the writing returns us to ourselves. We women have always done that, since we have no wives to protect our solitude.

MAY 5, 1996

More and more, I require solitude. For years I have been faithful to my journal and to enhancing my understanding of creativity and interconnectedness. Now my desire is to delve far beyond the academic knowledge I once confused with truth. I know how to find context, how to integrate seemingly disparate points of view and weave things together into a larger whole. In the months to come I'd like to return more often to the wordless center of that tapestry. It's a delicious paradox for a writer to be seeking a wordless place!

JULY 22, 1996

I wish to know life deeply, to integrate all that I've learned over the years. Last night at dinner I blurted out, "I don't give a damn about the World Wide Web! I'm annoyed with the constant barrage of information hurled into my office every day."

My practical business self then insisted, "It's important to keep an eye on technology and to monitor trends."

"Ah," the goddess whispered, "it's deep wisdom of the ages that the world needs now — a knowing beyond surface events. One can get lost in light, sound, and flashing images that entertain and distract."

I wish the world could sit in silence for a day and listen to the beat of the human heart, hear the music of the earth, and know that since humankind is blessed and cursed with the power of conscious choice, it is we who must decide to honor the feminine spirit within — we, and perhaps the spirit guides that are waiting to have their voices heard.

I want to reread my most cherished books instead of scanning today's Internet postings. I want to find wisdom threads among pages that have changed my life.

OCTOBER 3, 1996

I've come across an interesting article about sabbaticals. Researchers have found that after a sabbatical people quickly recoup the cost — and more — because of new skills, perspectives, and careers they develop while taking time off. I wish someone would pay me to take a sabbatical! Right now, time seems like the most precious commodity in world.

NOVEMBER 26, 1996 (IN A HOUSTON AIRPORT GATE AREA WHILE EN ROUTE TO A THANKSGIVING REUNION WITH TED'S FAMILY)

On the way to the airport this morning, while listening to NPR's *Morning Edition*, I nodded knowingly to a commentator's parody about the time spent saving time. Her message reminded me of a comment by Vietnamese peace activist Thich Nhat Hanh that sits perched above my computer: "Humankind's survival depends on our ability to stop rushing." Evidently, while I'm at my computer, I'm too busy to notice it, for although I can remember the gist of it I've never implanted it in my memory. I vow to read these words daily until I can recite them whenever I catch myself rushing!

I feel stronger and more centered now than I did a few months back when Ted was ill and depressed after cardiac surgery, and I was struggling to take care of me while supporting him. I've not fully recovered from the stress overload, however. I can't stand to read anything business related. Literature that interests me at the start of the day fails to hold my attention later on. Piles of mail, material as well as electronic, make me weary. I toss brochures I think I "should" read, and dump e-mail messages after just a cursory glance.

On the bright side, I have begun taking time to cook low-fat meals from fresh ingredients and to exercises regularly. An added bonus — I've lost the fifteen pounds I've been obsessed with for so long. I finally met a long-held goal: turning sixty while slender and fit.

MAY 24, 1998

In her book *Everyday Sacred*, Sue Bender writes of a friend who hurt her knee while on vacation with her husband. The rest of the week she could only hike with him very, very slowly. During one such hike, a photographer came up behind her and said, "You're noticing so many wonderful things." The woman replied, "I see these things because I can't walk very fast."

Sue prompts a realization about these past few trouble-filled years: without the gut-wrenching events, I might never have slowed my pace enough to SEE. Had things been smooth sailing all the way, I might not have focused on what truly matters. There's a certain irony in the discovery that stormy seas is what brought me at last to seek solitude. Now I guard my quiet moments, because I know they ground me enough to step out into the world mindfully.

Reflective Writing:

～I LEARNED that my craving for solitude intensified in my fifties. Now, in my early sixties, I've come to honor it by expending my energy carefully, preserving quiet times, and allowing the well to refill naturally.

～I RELEARNED that growth spirals, sometimes quite slowly, yet always lifting me beyond where I've been.

～I DISCOVERED the importance of balance — of moving into silence and back out into the world.

～I REDISCOVERED the notion that if more people slowed down enough to reflect on and profit from their experiences, our chances for survival would go way up. We might even learn to thrive!

～I REGRET that I spent so many years believing I couldn't afford to take time for reflection.

∿**I APPRECIATE** that my partner also understands my need for solitude, leaving me to my quiet morning musings by the pool and uninterrupted afternoons of reading and writing and watching the water.

∿**RIGHT NOW I FEEL** certain that perpetual busyness separates us from our wiser selves, stealing our sense of wholeness.

∿**AND I WILL** always take time to listen to the stirrings inside me so that I can regain my sense of who I truly am and long to be.

Invitation to Write

How does this experience connect with yours? How is it different? Do you have enough solitude in your life? What rhythms do you feel while moving inward and going out into the world? How do you achieve balance in your life? Can you remember a time when you truly enjoyed being alone? If you long for solitude, how might you create it? Where do you go to find yourself?

Here are a few quotes to inspire you:

"*Sometimes, as I sit listening quietly within, it seems as if the very air in the house has been transformed...a hush of tranquillity, an attitude of devotion filling every room.*"
— Judith Duerk

"*I always forget how important the empty days are, how important it may be sometimes not to expect to produce anything....I am still pursued by a neurosis about work inherited from my father. A day where one has not pushed oneself to the limit seems a damaged damaging day, a sinful day. Not so!*"
— May Sarton

"*When we exist at the core of ourselves, we're departing from how we normally exist. We're bringing the heart, mind, body, and soul into focus and being present with them in a particular way: doing it on purpose, doing it with unconditional acceptance, and doing it with deep attentiveness.*"
— Sue Monk Kidd

"*Blessed solitude has become very important to me. I find that when I have a day alone, I just revel in it, indulge in it, bathe in it. It's the most incredible luxury. That seems to come with the fifties.*"
— Ellen Burstyn

14

Embracing the Feminine

FROM ROSALIE'S JOURNALS

My journal entries are filled with notes on coming home to my self and remembering who I am at heart. I do not know if I was raised to be a "daddy's girl," expecting education and intelligence to lead to power and prestige, or if I decided early on that his life was more exciting than my mother's chosen vocation as a housewife. But for one reason or another, I turned away from women's ways of being, knowing, and relating until the early 1980s, when my feminine core cried out for recognition.

While harvesting, I came across entries filled with grief over the separation from my feminine soul, as well as stories of healing re-unions. Along with her return came all sorts of new understandings, such as equating the love of meaning with the masculine aspect of ourselves and the meaning of love with the feminine. See for yourself how feminine consciousness persisted in attracting my attention until, to retrieve her, I willingly entered the wound left by my rejection of her.

MARCH 1981

During a visit with my guides last night, I was a teacher of spirit. My heart was hammered and chiseled open, and I agreed to teach from a "place of full heart." Was it a future lifetime I had entered or did I meet an aspect of myself I have yet to acknowledge?

My guides also provided a picture of a tree laden with ripe yellow and red pears. Intuitively, I understood that I must pick the fruit and then serve the people. My soul evidently depends on me to teach from a state of ripeness and, in doing so, to demonstrate feminine principles. After all, what fruit could be more feminine than a pear?

I conclude this entry with information that moves through my pen and onto the page:

Be with discipline, dignity, devotion, and delight. Dare to see as God sees. Hold passionately to "good" and "wholeness" as God's law. Realize that matter is not the reality, but rather one aspect of reality. When you align your energy field to resonate with wholeness, you reflect God consciousness.

FEBRUARY 1981

I am beginning to understand that a woman's journey is a quest for vision. Truths once taken for granted blur and disappear. Answers that previously satisfied no longer hold meaning. Women's survival requires fresh myths and new meanings — in other words, a full-blown exercise in creativity.

MAY 1981

In allowing the experience of myself to unfold, I have come to believe less in coincidence and more in my own initiative and intention. I wait less and act more. I am not as charming as I used to be. Nor do I place faith in being in the right spot at the right moment, whereas I used to believe I magically backed into whatever was right for me. Taking myself more seriously, I accept increased responsibility for my destiny.

MAY 1981

As I surrender my compulsion to understand, I seem to know more. I used to pride myself on quoting concepts and being intellectual. Now my heart, although inexperienced, wants at least 51 percent of the vote.

JUNE 1982

I awoke realizing that I had been schooled during the early morning hours. The lesson was this:

Surrender to the joy of being. Surrender to the joy of sharing. Invite others into their unique expressions of joy and creativity. Embrace joy with arms outstretched.

I want to teach others about surrender, but I am not yet prepared to do so. First, I must gather more experience.

APRIL 1985

Being in a reciprocal relationship with my guides feels like a game of cosmic catch. Sometimes I toss the ball by asking for information; other times I catch the ball unaware that I am even playing! Intent on initiating a round of cosmic catch, I now ask: What is important for me to know about balance?

It is always a balance between seriousness and playfulness, humility and rapture, surrender and expansion. Trust in your own experience. Trust in grace. Trust in timing. Trust in wisdom. Trust in the source.

FEBRUARY 1992

For most of my life I have gravitated toward relationships in which I repressed my spirit — appearance mattered most, I denied my depths, and love was conditional. The civil war is over!

FEBRUARY 1992

Affirming each day that all is in divine order feels as smooth and rich as honey. Each time I remember to adopt an attitude of ease, I become an extension of divine order.

APRIL 1992

I want to experience the power of attraction, the ease of manifestation, the fleeting bliss known to my cells since before I was born. Adapting to familial expectations, I have led too narrow a life. Now, as I surrender to honesty, I feel as though my family roots have been pulled up and cosmic roots are the only ones anchoring me to the earth.

MAY 1992

Trusting my body to reveal truths is the feminine way. Making peace with my body after decades of abiding by my intellect is a homecoming. I have been training my mind to wait in the wings as I breathe and relax, affirming my intuitive perceptions as if they were precious gems. Dare I extend 51 percent of the vote to my body's wisdom each time I need to make an important decision? How is this possible when not so long ago I assigned 51 percent to my heart? Maybe mathematics is changing!

MAY 1992

I explored the nearby meadows today, accompanied by the five neighborhood dogs. Together, we walked beside the small brook, the dogs stopping to slurp gallons of fresh, cold water. Coming upon a patch of soft grass, I lay down and sent out appreciation to the nature spirits for their ongoing care of our planet. Soon afterward, the following words sprang into my consciousness:

> *Continue to experience yourself as an offering. Know that we receive you as an offering of love and receptivity.*

I breathed deeply, recalling an interlude earlier in the day when I had taken a shower, shaved my legs, applied skin lotion to my entire body, and stretched out in a sunny area of the bedroom, offering myself to spirit. Then I emptied myself of the need to produce anything and filled myself with the recognition that reserving time to be an offering was enough. For minutes on end I merged my light with divine light.

AUGUST 1992

While sipping coffee in bed this morning, I reminisced about will. After deciding to move from Maine to New Mexico, I had focused my will to locate a house, and then to settle atop El Salto Mountain. Now, a year later, I am enjoying a softer, more flexible relationship with my will, for I trust myself as well as the universe. Native

Americans believe that to receive guidance one must be a hollow tube, and indeed, I am finding that as I make way for emptiness, I experience fullness. I desire to be a colorful empty tube!

SEPTEMBER 1992 (IN BALI, INDONESIA)

After two weeks of dancing four hours a day, I'm pregnant with insights. I actually have a sense of what Sun-au You, my eighty-year-old teacher, means when she has me move as if flirting with the gods. When I remember that the dancer resides in every cell of my body, rather than solely in my mind, I am able to perform complex movements with ease. While I focus my intention to connect with the heart of each movement, coordination comes naturally — human body expressing divine rhythm, human self and essence self united!

SEPTEMBER 1992

After dancing with Bali's moonless night sky and "flirting with the gods" while practicing the ancient steps of a woman's ritual dance, I watched these lines flow from my pen:

> *Breathe with ease.*
> *Be at ease.*
> *Enjoy your body.*
> *Embody the dance.*
> *Invite movement to be your entrance into eternity.*

OCTOBER 1992

The more I teach soul empowerment and the spiritual foundations of creativity, the more precious my unfolding feels. This experience calls upon me to be attentive, awake, and alone.

Lately, I have less and less need to defend myself. I am letting go of my desire to be right as well as my desire to know.

NOVEMBER 1992 (IN ENGLAND)

The call to silence demands that I devote more time to reflection and contemplation. It's not that I feel antisocial, but rather that I'm drawn to inner listening, inner movement, "indwelling" states. I am

more compelled to create silence for myself than to go to histori-
cal sites, brush up on my British history, or visit shops.

Who is the "I" that will become "me"? The roles of lover, mother,
daughter, granddaughter, and friend are giving way to a more
universal mode of being. Whatever form that might take, I wish to
be present for the untethering and re-forming.

DECEMBER 1992

Many women I know have been speaking of the power inherent in
maintaining "virginal space." Married friends, for instance, talk
about the need for time away from their husbands, time to honor
their inner spaciousness, a retreat from masculine approaches to
problem solving. It's almost as if we women instinctively recognize
the importance of frequently removing ourselves from relationship
in order to be handmaidens to our consciousness. Living by myself
guarantees this devotion.

My guides have reinforced my turning inward, explaining:

*As you become more familiar with the experience of indwelling,
you gift people with your presence. Grace awaits. If you do not
allow time and space for your own immersion, which precedes
emergence, who will?*

JANUARY 1993

I have been pursued by my soul since 1977, the year Mike died. Before his death I was not on a journey for meaning; now I desire to be
with people who speak truth and are able to ground their spirituality in their bodies. My dearest friends remind me to ground my
"cosmicity" in the ordinary.

FEBRUARY 1993

A friend just told me of a woman who decided to take a year off to
listen to her dreams. Surely, such a journey fosters wholeness of
heart. The rewards are measured in delight, connectedness, and
creativity rather than career, prestige, and money.

FEBRUARY 1994

I am slowly beginning to sort out this soul-shaping process. First, information arrives as blink truths that cannot be denied. Once I have incorporated this guidance into my life, I seem to access another dimension: guides and teachers infuse my consciousness with their frequencies. Recently, I received information downloaded directly from the source, to which I, in turn vowed to serve as a resource.

MARCH 1994

My soul's vocation is to usher others into their fullness so that they can embrace their own magnitude. This is a process of re-awakening and remembering. Always the guides and teachers assist as personality gradually gives way to essence.

APRIL 1994

It is impossible to live my spirituality part-time. Clinging to security in any form seems an affront to my soul.

More and more I realize that there is no right or wrong, only that which is *IN* alignment or *OUT OF* alignment with my soul. What would happen if families, communities, or entire cultures began to reinforce each member's soul destiny? How would things change if we treated every baby as a messenger from eternity with a destiny of its own that contributed to the destiny of all, as well as that of the earth and other planets? What if we were all reminded to express divinity daily? I do believe that is the function of therapy, friendship, and even marriage.

MAY 1995

It is a time of questioning. Yesterday I agreed to participate in a sweat lodge ceremony that my neighbor planned. Two women drove in from California and, without my knowledge, were charged a fee to take part in the sacred prayer ritual. As if that were not shocking enough, one of them said she had no intention to participate; she had come only to be with her friend, who was interested in attending.

While chiding myself for being judgmental, I realized that I desire to sit with women of integrity who are clear in their intention, who are weaving rather than being woven, who speak from a well of truth, and who dwell in the wisdom place. Here's another resolution: I will never again take part in a sweat lodge ceremony that requires payment for participation. To me, a sweat is an offering, an honoring, a time to pray — not a money-making venture.

JUNE 1996

I am teaching people how to be lovers of their souls. Both my work and my worth are about being WITH love, not necessarily IN love.

JUNE 1996

Things my muse has always told me:

- To listen — especially at night when the house is still
- That truth lives in my gut
- To trust her goodwill along with my own
- That she is available to comfort me, guide me, inspire me as long as I remember to call her
- To honor my origins as well as the present
- That the future, which issues forth from the past and the present, is up to me
- To trust in love's power to heal, and to remember that love leads to intimacy and immensity opens onto infinity
- To remember that my days on earth matter, because I am a blessing and life is sacred
- To value my inner little girl
- To be aware of how I treat others, because actions mirror the soul
- That loving, regardless of the personal consequences, adds to humanity's consciousness of light
- To retreat into silence for a while each day
- To appreciate the sacred hidden within the daily routines of life
- To see with God's eyes and forgive with God's heart

JUNE 1996

Leading a life with soul takes discipline. I must decide how to use my time, talents, and truth.

JUNE 1996

The more I think about an experience I had two nights ago, the more I tumble the ideas around in my head like stones in a rock polisher. The psychotherapist in me warns that if I share this information with others I could be institutionalized!

Although my perceptions were dreamlike, the experience did not take place in a dream. Rather, it occurred in another space-time dimension I must have traveled to transphysically and, in the way of the feminine, I absorbed the information on a cellular level. At the start I am in a hospital room with an unfamiliar man who I can tell is trying to die. He is surrounded by family and friends, all pleading with him to stay alive. I know none of them; I simply witness the family dynamics and the resistant energy.

Approaching the dying man, I realize that he is between worlds, attached to neither his present life nor his passage into the after-life. Intuitively, I sense that he has forgotten the blueprint of his soul — his "geometric light shape" —and hence is stalled between dimensions, unable to decide between living or dying.

Unlike the others in the crowded room, I am unattached to his decision. My assignment is simply to remind him of his energetic blueprint. Instinctively, I merge with his guides and request the necessary information. Then I see a snapshotlike sequence of the geometric shape of his cells and am instantly aware that he remembers his blueprint. Not knowing of his decision, I leave the room and head for the hospital door wondering if the original last rites of the Catholic Church reminded dying people of the geometric blueprint of their souls.

At the moment, I cannot fathom the meaning of this encounter. All I know is that in this instance, as in others, I was out of body in search of information. Curiously, few people know of my nightly curriculum.

(Note: In July 1998, my friend Merrill died of a heart attack. When I heard the news, I automatically checked in with his guides to see if he had remembered his cosmic blueprint; it seemed the most natural thing in the world to do. He had — a discovery that brought joy.)

JUNE 1997

I was invited by phone to be one of the cameo presenters at the Creative Problem Solving Institute (CPSI), where I have taught for almost twenty summers. When asked if I would design a session on grief, I wanted to decline, saying, "But I'm not there anymore. I'm designing workshops on soul empowerment and intuition, not grief." But since this year was the twentieth anniversary of Mike's death, I replied, "I'll do it only if we name the session Grief As Shadow Side of Creativity," half hoping they would refuse. "And there's one more requirement," I added. "It will have to be an experiential sharing of our love for those who no longer reside in this dimension."

"You're in charge of this one, Rosalie!" I was told.

I suppose it's full-circle time, I thought to myself as I hung up. I have lived through grief, which initially convinced me that my creativity was dead, too. Then as time passed and I began shepherding others through grief, I was delighted to find that creativity led the way.

So I decided to open the workshop by honoring Mike as my teacher and by inviting participants to name their currently inspirited teachers. Yes, I am determined to guide this workshop not as a "daddy's girl" focused on form and intellect, but by honoring my inner experience.

JUNE 1997 (AT CPSI)

The cameo presentation is over. At first I was nervous, afraid that no one would come. But over a hundred people filled the room, most of them arriving late. Who wants to come early for grief?

While speaking, I patted my heart frequently, reminding myself that only a community can contain the depths of human grief and that this was indeed a community. Best of all, I talked about love and soul and the need to reinvest in love while grieving. How relieved I am that grief is no longer the shadow side of my creativity!

JULY 1997

During a five-day writing retreat on Maine's Monhegan Island, I was assigned the topic of parents and spirituality. I surprised myself with all that I had to say:

∿ I wish my parents had taught me about a living spirituality instead of their restrictive Baptist orientation to life.

∿ I wish my parents had taught me that spirituality is a way of being twenty-four hours a day.

∿ I wish Christmas had been an occasion for demonstrating reverence and thanksgiving instead of overspending and overeating.

∿ I wish my parents had accompanied me to Sunday school and church.

∿ I wished my parents had taught me that God is love and we are an extension of God's heart.

∿ I wish my parents had taught me that we are all Bibles when we speak our truth.

∿ I wish my parents had invited spirituality to supper each night rather than having the minister eat with us once a year.

∿ I would like to teach my parents that nature is adorned in the clothing of spirituality; that music is the sound of spirituality, art is the heart of spirituality, relationships form the ground of spirituality, words are the breath of spirituality, children are the future of spirituality, kindness and the will to do good reflect the spirit of God, silence is the promise of spirituality, and love is the energy that connects all beings, actions, events, and lifetimes. Wrapped in a circle of love, we become linked to our goddess self and the goddess selves of one another.

JUNE 1998 (AT CPSI)

It is past midnight and I am unable to sleep. Two hours ago I was named one of three recipients of the prestigious Creative Leadership award.

When my name was announced, I thought I was hallucinating. But there was Alison on one side of me and Michael on the other, squeezing my hands and urging me to step up to the stage amid the wild applause. My heart did not feel wide enough to take in this distinction bestowed so generously by my colleagues. When I walked back to my seat, hugs greeted me everywhere. Young men and women I had taught beamed at me. As before, Alison and Michael held my hands, only this time they hung on until I stopped shaking.

My soul feels seen and honored at last. What's more, the two other recipients were also women, reminding us all that the entire night was dedicated to feminine leadership. Our place is here; our time is now.

JULY 1998

This afternoon another woman writer asked me, "Do you ever ask for guidance that you are not prepared to follow?"

I smiled, shook my head, and replied, without thinking, "Not anymore. I prefer to surrender to the ease of evolution." Tears filled my eyes as I realized that no matter where I am my inner compass points to the magnetic direction of my soul.

Consecrating my life to alignment with my soul's purpose means I have no guarantees, no traditional loyalties, and a comparatively sketchy vita. My service solely entails acting as a resource for the source.

AUGUST 1998

Apparently, my education is still not complete. More guidance surfaced this afternoon:

> One of the ways to entrain your soul is through daily communion amid the beauty of nature's offerings. Fill your senses with the fragrance of flowers, the taste of salt water on your lips, the songs of brightly colored winged ones, the vibrating footsteps of those who have walked a similar path.
>
> Remember, you have carried the vibrations of a mystic for more than this lifetime. Embodiment challenges the mystic to experience and express gratitude each day while living in the world. A cloistered milieu is not your habitat this incarnation, familiar as it is. Daily bridging your human consciousness with what lies beyond it is part of your soul's purpose. Solitude and devotion are merely your foundations.

Continue to say yes to the mystery. Surrendering humility, move into high heart, the space of majesty. You will have reentered the domains of light when mystery and majesty unite.

This feels like a lifetime of work! How do I put legs on it all? I sigh and answer, "By beginning."

Reflective Writing:

∾ **I LEARNED** how gradually my intuition has replaced my intellect in daily dealings with the world.

∾ **I RELEARNED** how dutifully I accepted the cultural imperative to think, behave, and progress like a man, and how hard I have worked to claim my own ways. Not until the birth of my daughter, when I was thirty years old, did I begin this quest, spurred on by the desire to let her grow in her own ways.

∾ **I DISCOVERED** how much I wrote about the inner landscape of my soul. My intuition was not silent or silenced after all — I had simply not been educated in honoring it!

∾ **I REDISCOVERED** my fascination with women's ways.

∾ **I REGRET** that I didn't become conscious years before.

∾ **I APPRECIATE** the patience this "growing in" asks of us, and the many times I was tempted to give up because I lacked models. I am grateful that women stepped in to nudge me into consciousness.

∾ **RIGHT NOW I FEEL** excited thinking about the unexplored territory that lies ahead, and about offering my stories so that other women will know they are not alone.

∾ **AND I WILL** explore the unmapped turf. All the while, I vow to approach my intuition in ever fresh ways.

Invitation to Write

What threads count in your relationship with feminine consciousness? What brought you joy? What did you relinquish? What decayed? Who were your teachers — did you have feminine role models? What do you wish to say to others about your journey into feminine consciousness?

If any of the following quotations excite you, record them in your notebook and, using them like paints on a palette, fill in the contours of all that you are, including the highly esteemed masculine and the long suppressed feminine.

"The task for today's woman is to heal the wounding of the feminine that exists deep within herself and the culture." — Maureen Murdock

"My role as a feminist is not to compete with men in their world — that's too easy, and ultimately unproductive. My job is to live fully as a woman, enjoying the whole of myself and my place in the universe." — Madeleine L'Engle

"There is a void felt these days by women and men who suspect their feminine nature, like Persephone, has gone to hell. Wherever there is such a void, such a gap or wound, healing must be sought in the blood of the wound itself.... So the female void cannot be cured by conjunction with the male, but rather by an internal conjunction, by an integration of its own parts." — Nor Hall

"The road back home in some ways is the road back into the body, a time to get to know ourselves again on an interior, almost cellular level." — David Whyte

PART IV

Celebrating the Bounties

Conserving the Old and Propagating the New

You've returned from the fields and weighed your harvest, no doubt focusing on the richness of your life's journey. Now it is time to pick through the sheaves you have bundled, and even some you've not yet bunched together, for material worth perpetuating in one form or another. Here you will find ideas for preserving portions of your crop and for disseminating the seeds you have collected.

15

Preserving Prize-Winning Memories

*C*oming upon precious moments in an old journal is like spotting forgotten treasures while rummaging through a spare closet or a junk drawer. Turning to a page of images still vibrant with meaning, you may say aloud, "Oh, look what I've found!" Entries that evoke a response of this sort are well worth preserving in a notebook of their own or in a computer file reserved exclusively for prize-winning memories.

To make the most of these gems, be sure to leave space at the end of each one for describing the possibilities it holds for the future. Then in seasons to come, some of them may eventually work their way into memoirs, poems, essays, short stories, creative nonfiction, or plays. Others may end up on canvases, or in screenplays, or choreographed into body movements. If nothing else, they can be turned into a memory scrapbook to share with family and friends.

Here are segments from our "evergreen" collections to help you get started. As always, borrow freely from these examples, adapting whatever prospects for the future might apply.

FROM ALISON'S COLLECTION:

SEPTEMBER 10, 1975

Today I began a creative writing group as part of a middle school choice program to help kids explore their special interests. I sat on the floor in a circle with nine middle school girls (no boys chose this group), wondering what would happen. At first the girls were stiff and shy, not knowing what to expect. I told them how extra-ordinary I thought they were because they had chosen to be in a writing group. They seemed to accept that, signaling agreement with their eyes.

Who are these girls? I can't wait to find out! Quiet Ginny — dark intelligent eyes, shy, serious, following you every step of the way, hanging on to your every word — a teacher's dream! Dark, self-confident Emelia. Black, sexy Queenie, not sure she really wants to be there, but going along with it all; if it had smelled like a regular English class, she would have put on the proud, defiant facade I've seen her wear in the hallways. Vibrant Kelli, ready to go, volunteering thoughts easily. What a joy it is to EVOKE rather than TEACH!

SEPTEMBER 17, 1975

This afternoon I took over another teacher's class so she could leave early. As soon as the bell rang, the Spanish teacher on the other side of the room's back wall began playing Latin music blaringly loud. At the same time, a small mischievous-looking boy began chattering to his buddy. I asked him to stop talking because there was already enough noise and the other kids couldn't hear the information they needed for an upcoming test on the method of inquiry. "But listen, Mrs. Strickland, the walls are singing!" Wow, I thought, a poet who's attuned to the theory of singing walls!

I ended the day in a second teacher's class. The poetry lesson she'd left was awful, so instead of following her lesson plan, I told the kids how I felt about poetry — how I'd been scared off from it by an old dried-up teacher in elementary school. I then started reading them selections I like from a book of contemporary poetry. After that, I asked them to read me verses from their textbook, whereupon the class came alive.

Spotting a rebellious-looking girl in the back row, I felt a flash of recognition pass between us: I'd thrown her out of my class yesterday when she had wandered in without a hall pass to see a boy. Now, the resentment gone, she asked, "Want to read my poem? I wrote it myself." I read her poem to the class; the writing was rough, yet deep for an eighth grader, asking where memories go. She used space-travel metaphors to explore possible answers. She saw I really liked her poem, so after class she lingered and we talked about writing. She smiled; I smiled. Amazing...this tough kid and I coming together over a poem!

Possibilities:

I cherish these simple entries from my days as a young teacher. They remind me of the person I once was and, in a sense, still am although I now work with grown-up writers. These entries will stay in the "keeper" file on my computer until I am called to write on the notion that poetry is everywhere and sharing it can dissolve barriers.

NOTE ON BACK COVER OF JOURNAL FINISHED SEPTEMBER 30, 1992

This morning I heard the Dalai Lama interviewed on National Public Radio's *Morning Edition*. The correspondent asked him how it felt to return to his native Tibet after so many years of exile. The essence of his response: No big deal! "I've become a citizen of the planet," he replied, his voice hinting at a peace-filled smile, "and I'm at home ANYWHERE I FIND HUMAN SMILES."

Possibilities:

I remember exactly what I was doing while listening to this program — knotting a scarf around my neck while standing before a mirror in my bedroom at the retreat center where I often worked. I had been homesick after days on the road, and the Dalai Lama reminded me that I could always find a way to feel at home. I will write more about this, perhaps in an essay.

SEPTEMBER 29, 1993

I saw her in the early morning as I stood with our luggage waiting for curbside checking at the airport in Phoenix, Arizona. The desert air cool and dry, clear sunlight bouncing off nearby hills. An old woman smiling brightly at the porter who checks her bags. Obviously, not a typical little old lady. She wears a sheepskin vest with a horse head burned into the rough leather on the back, beige jeans that hug her slender body, beige Rockport walking shoes, and a wide-brimmed straw hat trimmed with a lace band that is tied in a big bow at the back. As she leans over her steamer trunk and large, soft suitcase, it's clear her back's curved with age. She carries a shopping bag bearing an expensive-looking logo shaped like a crest. The bag's filled with gaily wrapped gifts. The porter calls out, "Wheelchair!" and when it arrives, she pops into it, placing her shopping bag on her lap. Her deeply tanned, weather-worn face still beaming, she's whisked away.

I spot her later in a long line at the Delta counter, still smiling, still in her wheelchair, chattering with the porter as he pushes her forward each time a space opens up. I wonder where she's going and what takes her there. The large trunk and big suitcase suggest that wherever she's going, she intends to stay awhile. Or wherever she's been, she's been there for some time. She radiates happiness. I decide she's heading out on a long-anticipated journey that's taking her somewhere she's eager to go.

I point her out to Ted. "What a feisty old woman she is!"

"She looks like a Westerner who knows the land."

We speculated about the travel tales she could tell of days before jets whisked people from one place to another in hours. We guessed she was a great storyteller.

Possibilities:

When I found this forgotten entry, the entire experience burst back into my awareness. I could see that old woman clearly. I could also see the table in the airport coffee shop where I sat capturing images of her in my journal. All the details returned — bright Arizona sunlight streaming through the window, steaming coffee with cream beside me, the man reading a newspaper at the table to my right.

One day, I might bring her alive in a story about an indomitable woman with an adventurous spirit who relishes her life till the end. For now, I want to carry her image as a reminder that old age can bring joy and adventure. Her radiant smile and easy way with the tall man pushing her wheelchair makes her a woman I intend to keep around as a "travel companion."

NOVEMBER 29, 1996 (WHILE FLYING OVER THE PLAINS OF TEXAS)

Glancing down, I see that my legs are turning into my father's! Between the tops of my socks and the bottoms of my jeans, four inches of skin lie exposed — freckled, traced with fine intersecting lines I'd never see with my glasses off, decorated with light brown spots just like those on my father's legs when he was an old man. Both his and mine were etched by the sun during countless hours spent walking on beaches. They're not my mother's legs, although they're shaped like hers, for my mother never went out in the sun. Even as she lay dying, her ninety-three-year-old legs were white and smooth. Me? I'll take the spots, since each walk by the water has been worth it, especially those I took with my father.

Possibilities:

This piece makes me want to collect more snippets of my life. I could fit them together into a mosaic of memories with accompanying photographs or drawings. Perhaps a short story will begin with a woman gazing at her legs and remembering her father.

FEBRUARY 26, 1997

Today Ted and I got up early to spend the morning playing with our grandchildren, Adam and Anna, in a sun-washed St. Petersburg park. Adam loved spinning on the tire swing, getting dizzy for fun, staggering when he got off, and giggling while trying to walk straight. When Anna's turn ended, she refused to let Adam have another ride. "My swing!" she declared with the determination of a two year old.

What would you expect to happen next? A sibling battle royal, of course. But not so for Adam and Anna. "No, Anna," Adam answered softly, "it's the park's swing, but it's OK for you to have it for now." Then he trotted off happily to play on the slide. It amazes me how gentle and noncombative this spunky kid is with her.

When Anna tired of the swing, Ted took her to see the gulls. Spying one resting on the grass, Anna looked up at Ted and asked, "What's the matter him?" Apparently, she'd never seen a bird sitting around before. To her, Grampy Ted has become "P-Ted." I am "Grammy," although each time she says the word I think she's talking about my mother!

While driving home, I realized I'd remained present the entire morning. No drifting off to ponder business issues or make mental "to do" lists. Just drinking in a series of precious moments deserving to be savored. Growing down.

Possibilities:

This piece definitely goes into the book of memories I want to write for my grandchildren. I'd like Adam and Anna to know of the amazingly loving relationship they had in early childhood and that they were the ones who at long last taught me to live in the moment.

JUNE 9, 1998 (AFTER A CHOLESTEROL SCREENING AT THE WELLNESS CENTER)

This morning, when the nurse pulled on latex gloves, skillfully inserted a needle in my arm, drew a vial of blood, and deftly popped the disposable needle into the small red receptacle labeled "Hazardous Bio-Waste," I remembered a time when we humans weren't so afraid of one another's blood.

Possibilities:

There's a starkness to this short piece. Reading it aloud, I foresee turning it into a prose poem. It could easily be part of an essay, too. I have no plans for an anthology of flashbacks suggesting that the world's gone to hell and we're all close behind; but since volumes reeking of cloyingly sweet moments bore me, I'll keep pieces like this for balance.

FROM ROSALIE'S COLLECTION:

JUNE 1991

A conversation with Sister Anita, one of the older nuns at Bay View Convent, touched my heart. It began when she asked, "Rosalie, is CHANNELING a new word?"

"I think the word has been fashionable for about ten years," I answered eagerly, hoping to invite more conversation.

She looked deeply into my eyes and said, "Is it similar to the old-fashioned way of praying? You remember, how we all used to do it together?"

"Essentially the same," I replied, reaching out to touch her hand.

"So, channeling is a way of uniting with God?" she asked, giving my hand a gentle squeeze.

"That's been my experience," I said softly.

"Here we are taught to attend always to the plurality — oneself and others. There is no such state as I."

"It's very different in the world I live in," I replied with sadness.

"And difficult," she added quietly.

Sister Anita continued as if we were old friends: "When I am dying, I want no distractions. I refuse to have sisters around watching; they can pray in the parlor. I wish to be totally absorbed in God's approach."

Tears filled my eyes, for I had never heard death described as "God's approach." Then I giggled at the image of the other sisters banned from her room and ordered to pray in the parlor.

I thanked Sister Anita for her thoughts and told her, "I, too, desire to live each day ready for God's approach."

She reached out her arms and hugged me. Then holding my hand, she said, "You are a sister at heart even if you do wear outlandish clothes!"

My heart is touched by Sister Anita's friendship and confidence.

Possibilities:

I plan to interview other nuns on the subject of spirituality. I'd like to integrate their responses into a book about the many ways in which women worship.

JUNE 1992

Kelli-Lynne confided to me this morning that she feels nervous about flying to Maine alone. Even though she is now a high school graduate, some aspects of our relationship have not changed.

"Do you think my plane will be all right and not get hijacked, Mom?" she asked.

"Are you really nervous about that happening, Kelli-Lynne?" I replied.

"No, but lots of other kids worry about that stuff."

"How about if I put angel wings around the plane so you will be safe — would that help you feel better?"

"How about putting angel wings around my whole body."

"Sure, how many would you like?" I asked, aware that beneath our playfulness was a serious conversation.

"As many as it takes. I'm being practical, Mom."

"Thanks for telling me you were nervous and asking me to help."

"That's what we do for each other, Mom."

My heart felt warm. We have learned that we can count on each other, and for that I feel blessed.

Possibilities:

Most of the time, Kelli-Lynne acts intelligent and in control. Yet every now and then she exhibits what Buddhists refer to as "beginner's mind." I enjoy her most when she believes in magic as much as medicine. I will use this piece in a scrapbook of verbal exchanges I plan to compile for her. A few notches beyond a "baby book," this volume will chronicle my daughter's journey into womanhood in her own words. Perhaps I'll give it to her when she becomes a mother.

MARCH 1996

For years the vigilante energy of the Greek goddess Echo has strengthened me whenever the feminine has been neglected, abused, or silenced. She has reminded me to protest against injustice, to protect myself and those I love, even to kill if that appears to be the only recourse for justice. She encouraged me to protest against the Vietnam and Gulf Wars; to serve as a leader in Take Back the Night demonstrations against the sexual abuse of women; to step forward and bring down the American flag during an ERA demonstration; to speak out on behalf of my daughter's safety. Yes, she transmits vigilante vitality and more.

Echo keeps me defended. It is she who encourages me to compete against men, using any strategy to win. It is she who keeps me in the retaliatory role of Amazon. It is she who deafens me to the possibility that men are as capable of change as women. It is she who claims me when I stomp off in rage instead of recognizing that the man I love is not the enemy.

As I evolve, my loyalty to Echo is coming under question. I desire to be a friend to her, to appreciate all that she has taught me, and to take back my vow of absolute obedience to her. In releasing my unconditional loyalty to Echo, I pledge to live in the here and now, all the while trusting in the possibility of peacemaking between men and women. I do so now in honor of Echo and myself so that we may each continue to grow in consciousness. So be it.

Possibilities:

The power of this entry moves me still. I plan to expand this piece for submission to women's magazines.

JULY 1996

For a month I have been affirming beauty — the beauty of nature as well as my inner beauty. Knowing from experience that affirmations build consciousness, I am receptive to beauty in ALL its forms.

I begin each day by walking on the Eastern Promenade in Portland and meditating on a large rock on the beach. Today, as I began my walk, I encountered an unshaven, disheveled old man retrieving returnable bottles from garbage cans. I felt initially repulsed by such a distraction on this beautiful morning, and then sad that anyone had to resort to garbage-picking for cash. We nodded to each other as I passed, hurrying along to avoid further contact.

Once at the beach, I mounted my meditation rock. As the sun added its warmth to the day, I closed my eyes and prepared to enter the quiet. Breathing softly, I began to energize beauty by remembering occasions when I was present for it and it was present for me.

A rough voice pierced my stillness. "Nice day, don't you think?"

Opening my eyes, I saw the garbage picker. "Can't he see I'm occupied?" I asked myself, annoyed by the intrusion. I shut my eyes again, but with my attention shattered, reentering the sacred circle of my consciousness felt impossible. After trying several times to return to the place of quiet mind and balanced heart, I gave up.

While heading for the tarred driveway that led back to my apartment, I spotted the man again. This time he approached me with one hand behind his back and waved. There was no way to avoid him. Yet, although no one else was in sight, I somehow felt safe.

"I have something for you," he announced loudly, "but first you must close your eyes."

"Right," I thought to myself. "You have one of those dirty bottles you've been collecting." Looking directly at him for the first time, I noticed that he appeared about sixty years old, was potbellied, and wore glasses. His clothes were typical Maine, minus the L.L. Bean look. Deciding that he was harmless, I closed my eyes as requested.

"Now, hold out your hands," he said.

"Are you sure this won't hurt?" I heard myself ask.

"You'll see," he replied, "but first hold out your hands."

I did as he asked and soon felt something skinny with a sharp edge in my left hand. Opening my eyes, I saw a long-stemmed red rose.

"Beauty to beauty," he said while ambling over to a gray pickup truck.

As he drove off I noticed, amid a myriad of bottles and garbage bags, a tall tin pail filled with red roses. "Thank you!" I hollered while his truck was still in view.

I will never know if he heard me, or if he has any idea about the profound lesson in judgment that he inspired. I will, however, be reminded of him each time I see a red rose.

The old adage is true: The teacher appears when the student is ready. Seldom have I been confronted so clearly with the split between my inner life and its outer expression. I wish I knew the name and address of the man who reminded me of beauty, because I would send him a thank-you note or maybe even this piece of writing.

Possibilities:

Rereading this story, I again feel humbled. I plan to revise it and submit it to a magazine that features material on spiritual growth.

APRIL 1997

Whenever we switch the clocks ahead to daylight saving time or back to standard time, my grandmother reminds me, with an air of someone who truly knows, that the world now agrees it is one time, such as 7 A.M., but by God's time it remains another, in this case, 6 A.M. Even though she is now ninety years old and we no longer live together — in fact, we live two time zones apart — she called me early this morning to remind me that no matter what the clocks say, God's time continues on as before, one hour earlier.

After my grandmother's call, I pondered what my life might be like if I lived by God's time. For one thing, I would be more present. For another, regrets about the past would be attributed to the flaws inherent in human time. On this day, as the world switches to daylight saving time, I prefer to join my grandmother in celebrating God's time.

Possibilities:

My grandmother is as down-to-earth as I am cosmic, yet we have loved each other unconditionally since I was born. This piece belongs in a book I'm currently brewing about grandmothers — their stories and their wisdom. I plan to give it to my grandmother on her ninety-third birthday.

16

Writing from Your Writing

As you have already discovered, your old journals hold many seeds waiting to sprout into new writing. Some will come to light in the sheaves you have bundled; others will spring into view as you compile your collection of most treasured memories. All these seeds can germinate into polished, publishable works if you apply the techniques introduced below.

Creating New Writing from Lists and Unfinished Sentences

Your collection of lists, together with the unfinished sentences you've completed, as described in chapters 3, 4, 5, and 6, can serve as rich fodder for new writing in your current journal or as pieces for sharing or publishing. See where the following strategies lead you.

Returning to your lists, use a line that intrigues you to launch into a new piece. Perhaps one of the places you've written in begs for description. Or maybe there's a narrative hidden in an event you have only alluded to.

Choose one item from your "big, bold life-changing choices" list (see page 58) and tell the whole story.

Pick a sentence you have finished. Use it as the first line of something new.

Pick another sentence you have finished and use it as your last line. Begin writing with this line as your destination, meandering along the way if you wish.

Randomly select three sentences you've finished and work them into an essay. Finding a relationship between seemingly unconnected themes will stimulate links you might not otherwise make.

Select three related sentences you've finished and write a piece incorporating them all. Writing the path that leads from one to another of them will help you discover more about this thread in your life tapestry.

Weave together a poem from phrases and short sentences.

Pick a recurring theme and write about it. Prepare a bundling of entries if you like.

After finding references to dragons in many of her journals, Alison wrote this piece at the end of a journal finished in December 1994. At the outset she asked herself this question to get her writing flowing: "What most wants to be said about dragons?"

REFLECTIONS ON DRAGONS

Dragons hide things, especially your voice. To find it, you must go deep, dig around, evoke it, tease it out. All the while, you must chase away the dragons guarding it. They know that if you find it, write it, name it, know it, they'll lose power, and that if this happens often enough they'll have to slither off and torment someone else. Why is this so? Because when you've found your voice, there's NOTHING left for them to hide from you.

Of course, they CAN sneak back, especially when you're so sure they're gone for good that you get lazy, lose your focus, and forget your intention. Soon after they take up residence in you again, the world dims and you begin to feel heavy, dense, and ordinary once more.

Dragons love impatience and perfectionism. Even when you write something thrilling, they'll convince you it's flawed. In the process, they'll devour your confidence and eat up your dreams.

Dragons crept in before you can remember. Eggs were laid under your crib. Hatchlings lurked in your nursery closet. As soon as they were old enough to slither about, fire-breathing creatures whispered you'd better be really good, well aware that you could never be good enough. They told you that what you did poorly mattered more than what you did well, and taught you to dwell on your mistakes while taking your successes for granted.

Properly handled, dragons can be useful. They help you grow stronger. Turn on them, face them, tell them you're onto them and the game's up. In fact, the moment you say they can't scare you anymore, they shrivel up, lose their fire, and slither away.

You know when they're gone — you feel lighter, the air's clearer, the light's brighter. Your eyes brighten, too. Smiles come more easily and laughter feels like a birthright. You're at ease in your skin. Your thoughts flow more freely. New connections pop and possibilities seem more viable. A dragon-free state is a great place to be in.

Just remember that they have one hell of a network and slink around the neighborhood watching and waiting for a chance to sneak back in. It's best to go on dragon patrol regularly and to keep on hand a supply of things they abhor, like laughter, gratitude, purpose, friends who cheer you on, and someone special who will rub your back when you're tired. Also float dreams over your bed — visions of what you want to create next, of a better tomorrow, and of a world where dragons have a more suitable game to play than sucking out your joy.

Answering Your Own Questions

The questions raised in your journals point out your most pronounced conundrums and curiosities. The answers you provide will show your growing wisdom. Your responses may take the form of either a private entry or something more public, such as an essay or a letter.

Choose a poignant question you've posed, perhaps in response to list #2 in chapter 4, and write it at the top of a blank journal page, along with the date of the original entry; then answer it, dating your response. As time goes on and your perspective changes, return to this page to record and date new answers. You could even ask your muse or your wiser self to respond to the question for you, then initiate a dialogue between your point of view and theirs.

Here are two questions Rosalie gathered from her early journals, together with answers she provided in June 1998. More answers may bubble up in the future.

OCTOBER 1981

As women, are we ever prepared for the reality of divorce?

JUNE 1998

I expected to outgrow clothes and some friends and even places, but not my husband. I wasn't ready for yet another grief cycle — one more round of letting go of dreams and a future with someone I once loved.

Ours is the first generation to accept divorce. Neither my mother nor grandmother could have prepared me for the lack of cooperation I experienced with the man I chose to marry.

Divorce is a battlefield. Husband and wife become adversaries, after which everything once shared is weighed in dollars and pension plans. Where is there room to exhibit feminine connection and goodwill? Certainly not in court!

My friends who are divorcing today are no better prepared than I was sixteen years ago. Although we have aged, illusions persist. I want to hug my women friends who stand on the threshold of a new life, and say, "Yes, there will be times of sadness and loneliness, but none to compare with the isolation you have endured by staying in a relationship that does not nourish your soul."

JUNE 1986

Have we all been taught to be less than ourselves?

JUNE 1998

Over and over again I listen to women complain about the codes of behavior they have adopted: "Don't brag," "Don't be cocky," "Don't be selfish," "Don't be too powerful," "Don't be greedy," "Don't be spoiled."

What does being spoiled mean, anyway? Does it mean asking for what I want and refusing what I don't want? I am more comfortable taking up physical space than I am while occupying emotional space.

Using an Entire List

Working with an entire list can flesh out your picture of the past and cross the threshold into a new tomorrow. Try these exercises to catapult you into the future.

Look over your list of regrets and things you whine about — or any collection of chief complaints you've found in your journals. Imagining what your existence would be like if you resolved these issues, write about a day in the new life you envision. What might happen if you were to start living *as though* these changes had taken place?

Review your list of sacred people, events, conversations, places, rituals, and activities. Assuming that at least one day a month could be filled with the sacred, plan your day. You may want to build in time for ceremonial music, food, or clothing. Can any of your everyday routines be converted *into* sacred practices? Who will you invite to join you? Remember, this is your fantasy, so you can extend an invitation to imaginary people, characters from books or movies, your muse, even someone who has died. Set up a monthly appointment with yourself to commemorate this sacred day.

Refer to your list of big, bold life-changing choices to write a short autobiography in celebration of your courage.

Alluding to the list of places you've written in, as well as your "I am a writer who..." and "I write to..." lists, compile your history as a writer. Arrange it chronologically, beginning with your earliest recollections of writing; geographically; or in a way that reflects your shifts in purpose.

Writing from Your Own Best Lines

Just as you can respond to brief quotes from other writers, you can grow new writing from quotes of your own. Return to your seed journal for irresistible quotes, or to any other collection of your most inspired thoughts. Then transplanting one onto a fresh page, consider it the first line of a prose poem, an essay, a short story, or a novella. See where it takes you.

Alison pulled the following quotes from her journals and transplanted them into her seed journal. She suspects that these will someday evolve into new writing.

> *"Life is a moment-by-moment miracle...yet how often we take it all for granted. Every day is a creation that's ours to make."*

> *"My sage plant's thriving. Thick with new growth, it's doubled its size in little more than a week when only a month ago I thought it might wither."*

> *"A crap detector is essential in this world. So, too, is a truth detector; without one, we're apt to fall too easily into cynicism."*

> *"Could it be that our most healing work is not to CHANGE who we are, but to truly BE who we are?"*

Writing from Your Omissions

Spans of time when you didn't write and incidents you left out are rich with possibility, for whatever you neglected to record remains alive *within* you. Expounding on the list of events you didn't write about or of regrets you omitted, or on other undocumented segments of your life may prove to be revelatory, if not healing. If you encounter resistance while revisiting these landscapes of your past, strive to write *beyond* it; the fruits of your labor may well be replenishing.

Here Rosalie finally begins writing about a five-month depression she experienced nearly a decade earlier. Giving voice to the experience helped place her suffering in perspective. She was able to forgive herself for not trusting her intuition and to acknowledge that depression was a teacher for her.

I do not want to write about my depression, although nine years have elapsed since it called me to truth. All my other experiences

of loss have been named and dated: my hysterectomy, Mike's death, my divorce, betrayals, family disintegration. Only this passage remains undescribed.

For about five months I had no voice. Sighs replaced words. Unblinking stares took the place of conversation. Private worries so occupied my attention that I could no longer think clearly. Meditation felt like a stranger; creativity was deadened. I'd convinced myself that my guides and teachers had dismissed me, and the pain of their desertion was unbearable.

I did not want to face the truth: my husband had betrayed me. Worse yet, I had colluded in the act by hanging on to his reassuring words of love, by agreeing to be lulled further into the illusion that I could trust the man I had married. Shame surrounded me and I felt shackled. I wanted only to sleep. And forget. And die.

One of my friends lovingly found the words that broke my trance: "Rosalie, your soul has been raped." My body responded with a deep, knowing sigh, aware that at last someone understood the depths of my grief.

Today I discovered a prescription for depression by prominent nerve specialist Dr. S. Weir Mitchell, writing in the early 1900s:

Live as domestic a life as possible.
Have your child with you all the time.
Lie down an hour after each meal.
Have but two hours of intellectual life a day.
And never touch pen, brush or pencil as long as you live.

Had I lived in the early 1900s, I would not have survived depression.

Sharing Your Harvest

Once you have crafted your work into new journal entries, essays, articles, short stories, poems, a memoir, or perhaps the beginning of a novel, what can you do with it? Like any avid harvester, you can serve it up in celebration of the season. The type of feast you prepare is up to you. For example, you could assemble a mosaic of poetry, contemplative thoughts, or precious memories and run off copies of it for your family and friends. Using a scanner, you could add drawings or photographs. Creative possibilities abound!

Or you may decide to enter the traditional publishing world by submitting a book proposal to a literary agent who will then "pitch" it to publishers and negotiate a contract for you. Twelve to eighteen months after signing the contract, you can plan on seeing a published book.

You also have the option to self-publish your work. Because each year major publishing houses are bringing out fewer books by unknown authors and spending most of their advertising funds on celebrities and best-selling authors, a growing number of writers are choosing to publish their work independently. Contrary to popular opinion, self-publishing is a credible and affordable alternative to hiring a literary agent, finding a publisher, negotiating a contract, and waiting at least a year for the book to appear, all the while wondering how long it will remain in print. What's more, it gives you final say on the contents, design, title, and cover format, as well as greater control over the finances. Instead of a small royalty check delivered twice a year, you can realize more profit more often because you financed the project yourself.

Whether you keep the fruits of your harvest close to home or go commercial with them, know that because of your efforts your life will touch another's. One harvester who started out in search of personal insights combined several entries into a commentary that was eventually picked up by National Public Radio. Another gained the confidence to move ahead with a manuscript of literary fiction she had put aside. The material she uncovered in her journals brought the project alive again and, a few drafts later, into print.

17

Completing the Past and Imagining the Future

Important accomplishments deserve to be honored. Hence, in the spirit of recognition this chapter invites you to rejoice in your harvest and look ahead to a journey greatly enriched as a result of your labors. It begins with a completion ritual of thanksgiving. Next you will find a meditation to till the soil of self-expression within you — in terms of both your journal writing and other writing projects. The exercises following the meditation will help you prepare for another successful harvest in the future.

Thanksgiving: A Completion Ritual

Congratulations on completing your harvest! Now it is time for a thanksgiving ritual. Just as family and friends gather round the traditional Thanksgiving table to express appreciation for an abundant harvest, so can you spend a few quiet moments with your journals and then write up one last list — a gratitude list — in celebration of the succulent yield.

Here are the gratitude lists we compiled at the end of our first harvests. Perhaps they can help expand your repertoire of all there is to be thankful for at the close of your voyage into the past.

ROSALIE'S GRATITUDE LIST:

≫ I am thankful for having survived.

≫ I am thankful for the patience to persevere, which seemed to mushroom as time went on.

~I am thankful for friends who listened to the frustrations and satisfactions I felt upon reentering my journals.

~I am thankful for the insights I received at special places I visited while separating the grain from the chaff.

~I am thankful for my guides.

~I am thankful for the loving dogs that lapped my feet during the final stages of bundling the sheaves.

~I am thankful to Michael, my partner, who recognized my need for silence and solitude as new understandings took root within me.

ALISON'S GRATITUDE LIST:

~I am thankful for that first urge to put pen to paper and begin a journal.

~I am thankful that I always returned.

~I am thankful for the growing presence of my muse.

~I am thankful for all the writers who encouraged me to add my voice to theirs.

~I am thankful that I will not have to write another whiny word about not taking my writing more seriously.

~I am thankful for Ted's absolute trust and faith in me, and the back rubs he so willingly gave after my hours at the keyboard.

Now it's your turn to come up with a gratitude list. When you have finished compiling it, put it where you can easily find it. Then when you begin your next harvesting venture, you will have the fruits of your first one to cheer you on.

Consulting with Your Muse
A Meditation

Consulting heart-to-heart with your muse can help you uncover plans she — and you — might have in store for your future. Some people call this practice "meditative journeying," or time traveling, to discover what's coming next. As before, read the meditation all the way through to get a sense of it before beginning your consultation.

◆ Relaxing your body, breathe gently into areas that need extra love and attention. Whisper silently to yourself, "I am a writer," relaxing your body even more. Then breathe into your heart and thank it for supporting your harvesting journey.

◆ Playfully invite your muse to join in the celebration. Surround her with gratitude, and ask if she has messages for you about your writing. Continue to breathe gently, relaxing ever more deeply.

◆ To learn about the time ahead, affirm your intention to experience your future self. Then ask your muse to open up the future to you.

◆ After treating yourself to another relaxing breath, settle into your future. Where are you? What time of day or night is it? What season is it? What are you writing? What excites you about your writing? Who are your companions? How is your muse supporting you? How are you sustaining your momentum as a writer? What gifts are you claiming? What themes are you writing about? What images, thoughts, and ideas are you focusing on?

◆ Remind yourself that you can journey as far into the future as you desire and that you can go there anytime you'd like to, remain there as long as you wish, and carry the seeds of tomorrow into the present. All of this is within reach.

◆ Now bring your awareness and breath back to the present moment. Breathing into your heart once again, fill it with even more love. Wiggle your fingers and toes, and stretch your body, all the while telling yourself that you can return to the future whenever you wish. Check in with your muse to see if she has more seed thoughts for you. Is there anything *she* needs from *you*?

◆ When your consultation feels complete, thank your muse for coming.

Where Do You Go From Here?

Now that you have celebrated the crops planted in previous seasons and glimpsed into the future, it is an ideal time to enrich the soil for your next planting. Do you have another journal nearby waiting to be filled, or ideas for writing you would like to develop? If so, roll up your shirtsleeves and begin to plan the cultivation process.

Here is an exercise to assist you in this task: Using images, thoughts, and ideas from your meditation, plan your writing future. Include the projects you hope to accomplish as well as the pieces you want to write. Draw up a list, or draft a mind map, as described on page 52, if you like.

Below are sample items from our plans for the future. Freely adopt whichever of them pertain to *your* prospects for the future.

ROSALIE'S PLAN:

~ I will challenge myself to speak out more, write articles, address larger groups of people, and be as outrageous as I actually am.

~ I will honor my need for silent, reflective time each day to fortify the courage it takes to tell my stories.

~ I will collaborate with others who share a covenant to write and create.

~ I will write more about projection in relationships — what I project onto others as well as what they project onto me.

~ I will write more about the purpose of evil, including when I deny its reality, when I acknowledge it, how I cope with it, and how I add to it.

~ I will write about the transformative relationship I am experiencing with my married daughter, especially how to share our stories without regressing into the too familiar roles of mother and daughter.

~ I will describe what happens when I tone down my exuberance to match the energy frequency of friends who are coping with illness, divorce, career disruption, or depression.

ALISON'S PLAN:

≈ I will join more writer's circles.

≈ I will write more about women writers I've never met who have changed my mind, inspired my heart, and given me courage to continue my work.

≈ I will write poetry.

≈ I will illustrate my journals.

≈ I will write more in celebration than in confusion.

≈ I will write about my tiny granddaughter, Zoe Karen Strickland, and how she touched so many lives during the few hours she visited us on earth.

≈ I will remember the Yiddish proverb "If you want to hear God laugh, tell God your plans," and stay open to the unexpected.

The Last Sheaf

According to customs practiced throughout the agrarian world, one sheaf of grain remains in the field until the end of harvesting season—vestiges, some say, of an early belief in the fructifying power of Corn Mother. In some cultures, an elaborate figure is made of the last sheaf of corn; in others, an image is formed from the last-standing wheat sheaf; in still others, the privilege of making the final cut is ceremonially granted to a young girl. In each instance the last sheaf symbolizes a passage: birth, entry into maidenhood, or crossing the threshold into a new season of life. Always, there is an offering.

ALISON'S OFFERING:

The process of harvesting my journals has taken me from writing about wanting to write more to coauthoring the book I've dreamed of ever since I read Barry Stevens's *Don't Push the River* in the late 1970s. When my life seemed to be falling apart, Barry's meandering memoir showed me an indomitable spirit at work — one that had carried her from the role of a doctor's wife in Hawaii before the bombing of Pearl Harbor to that of a well-known lay therapist working with renowned Gestalt therapist Fritz Perls at Esalen Institute in Big Sur, California.

It wasn't an easy trip. Before sharing suppers with Fritz in Big Sur country, Barry suffered through a mysterious illness that nearly impoverished her, and she worked at low-paying jobs to support herself. She didn't end up a bag lady or bereft of her children, as I feared I might by letting go of my safety nets. To the contrary, she became an ever more vibrant elder. I'll never forget her image on the cover —

round, earthy body in a billowing caftan, feet planted firmly in the sand, arms outstretched. Her gray hair is carelessly pulled back in a bun; her eyes look up to the sky. I suppose she's gone from earth now. But wherever she is, I hope she knows I wrote this book for her, because she told the truth about her journey.

My fondest wish is that you will gain courage to claim your creativity, and that as a journal keeper you will not only renew your commitment to writing but also let your words be heard, because *we need them*. Each human story honestly told enriches us all.

ROSALIE'S OFFERING:

I applaud Mary Catherine Bateson's words, "Writing has been the constancy through which I have reinvented myself after being uprooted." During the past four years, I have lived in four countries and, while residing in North America, in three different states. Each time, the decision to uproot was mine. Although I create community for myself wherever I live, no longer do a few close friends hold the day-to-day details of my history.

Not until the final week of putting this book together did I realize how often I wrote to promote peace. Sometimes I was confused and wrote to bring harmony to my thoughts. More often, I wrote to surround my heart with peace. And there were times I wrote to extend this peace into the places I was visiting.

For example, while celebrating my fiftieth birthday in Cyprus, I stood in an observation tower watching three lines of brown-skinned youths carrying rifles. The two outer columns of soldiers protected their partitioned borders while the middle one, the United Nations Peacekeeping Force, prevented the Greek Cypriots and Turks from attacking each other. Never before had I realized how fragile peacekeeping was. Knowing that my consciousness, too, had at times been partitioned and now was not, I wrote to mediate an amnesty accord. I am beginning to recognize that peace is joy at rest.

My prayer is that you celebrate your life by writing the journal entries, stories, and memories that only you can write. May you write yourself into radiance!

Resources

BOOKS

Baldwin, Christina. *Life's Companion: Journal Writing As a Spiritual Quest*. New York: Bantam Books, 1990.

Buzan, Tony. *The Mind Map Book*. New York: Penguin Books, 1996.

Goldberg, Natalie. *Writing Down the Bones: Freeing the Writer Within*. Boston, MA: Shambhala Publications, 1986.

Heart, Rosalie Deer. *Healing Grief: A Mother's Story*. San Cristobal, NM: Heart Link Publications, 1996.

Levoy, Gregg. *Callings: Finding and Following an Authentic Life*. New York: Harmony Books, 1997.

Phillips, Jan. *Marry Your Muse: Making a Lasting Commitment to Your Creativity*. Wheaton, IL: Quest, 1997.

Wycoff, Joyce. *Mindmapping*. New York: Berkeley Books, 1991.

ORGANIZATIONS

Creative Problem Solving Institute (CPSI)
Creative Education Foundation
1050 Union Road
Buffalo, NY 14224
Phone: 800-447-2774
Fax: 716-675-3209
E-mail: *cefhq@cef-cpsi.org*
Web site: *www.cef-cpsi.org*

The International Women's Writing Guild (IWWG)
PO Box 810, Gracie Station
New York, NY 10028
Phone: 212-737-7536
Fax: 212-737-9469
E-mail: *iwwg@iwwg.com*
Web site: *www.iwwg.com*

About the Authors

*R*OSALIE DEER HEART, an international consultant, teaches intuition enhancement, spiritual foundations of creativity, and writing workshops. She also facilitates soul empowerment workshops, spiritual journeys, and retreats with her partner, Michael Bradford. Rosalie is the author of *Healing Grief: A Mother's Story* and coauthor of *Soul Empowerment: A Guidebook for Healing Yourself and Others*. In addition to teaching at the Creative Problem Solving Institute in Buffalo, New York, she is president of Blessingway Books, an independent publishers' marketing and distribution cooperative based in Santa Fe, New Mexico. She is a member of The International Women's Writing Guild, Women of Vision and Action, and Maine Writers and Publishers. In her spare time she sculpts and snorkels.

*A*LISON STRICKLAND is a consultant, workshop leader, and writer who lives on the west coast of Florida with her husband, Ted Coulson. Together, they founded Applied Creativity, Inc. in 1982, and they currently delight in the company of their five grown children and two grandchildren. Alison teaches at the Creative Problem Solving Institute, where she developed The Writing Place, a circle for people who want to grow their creativity through writing. A member of The International Women's Writing Guild, she is the author of three published children's novels and numerous professional articles.

Order Form

QUANTITY	TITLE	AMOUNT
_____	*Harvesting Your Journals: Writing Tools to Enhance Your Growth & Creativity* ($15.95)	_____
_____	*Soul Empowerment: A Guidebook for Healing Yourself and Others* ($15.95) by Rosalie Deer Heart and Michael Bradford	_____
_____	*Healing Grief: A Mother's Story* ($14.95) by Rosalie Deer Heart	_____
	Sales tax of 6.875% for New Mexico residents	_____
	Shipping & handling ($3.00 for first book; $1.50 for each additional book)	_____
	Total amount enclosed	_____

Quantity discounts available on orders of 10 or more books

Please mail your order, together with your
name, address, and check or money order, to:

HEART LINK PUBLICATIONS
PO Box 31280
Santa Fe, NM 87594
800-716-2953

We Would Like to Hear from You

We are currently planning a second *Harvesting* collection filled with contributions from other dedicated journal keepers. If you feel inspired to share your discoveries, please send them to:

ROSALIE DEER HEART at
RDeerheart@aol.com
(PO Box 31280, Santa Fe, NM 87594)
> or

ALISON STRICKLAND at
ACIAlison@aol.com
(13498 Alpine Avenue N., Seminole, FL 33776)

To find us on the Internet, visit *appliedcreativityinc.com*

We also consult with individuals and groups. If you are interested in sponsoring or attending a *Harvesting* workshop, call us at 800-716-2953.